Hard Core Europe

Hard Core Europe

✦

A fact-based Reality—check of the Banana Rep*EU*blic

Ralph T. Niemeyer

iUniverse, Inc.

New York Lincoln Shanghai

Hard Core Europe
A fact-based Reality—check of the Banana RepEUblic

iUniverse books may be ordered through booksellers or by contacting:

iUniverse
2021 Pine Lake Road, Suite 100
Lincoln, NE 68512
www.iuniverse.com
1-800-Authors (1-800-288-4677)

Because of the dynamic nature of the Internet, any Web addresses or links contained in this book may have changed since publication and may no longer be valid.

The views expressed in this work are solely those of the author and do not necessarily reflect the views of the publisher, and the publisher hereby disclaims any responsibility for them.

ISBN: 978-0-595-49205-3 (pbk)
ISBN: 978-0-595-61006-8 (ebk)

Printed in the United States of America

To

Sahra, my all-above loved wife
from who I receive so much inspiration and encouragement.

Contents

IV. Warshipped: EU 'peace' missions

V. The August 11th—Dossier

VI. 50 more years?

Only by a media controlled by industries employing Lobbyists rather than Journalists is it possible to create a hype that may let a system that is that clearly governing directly against the interests of the people appear as being without alternative. Berthold Brecht used to say on occasion of the tank encountered uprising of workers in Eastern Germany in 1957 that if the government was not pleased with its people it did better to choose a 'different people'. Given the fact that the majority of Europeans are potentially disenfranchised with the EU's economic course and way of executing social control by a harsh regime axing civil liberties Europeans once had been proud of one after the other, Berthold Brecht's phrase could be filled with life rather soon.

One can hardly be anti-European these days, especially if one enjoys the benefits of a liberal society, the freedom of movement, the cultural diversity, the prosperity of the single market and human rights but one should be even more sceptical if one only hears about others enjoying all aforementioned while one-selves is excluded, and one should ask critical questions rather than allowing main-stream media to try to make one believe that nobody else but one-selves is to be blamed if one does not participate in such beautiful public life. One should, for instance, ask whether it is not a myth that everyone has the same chances to live a happy, healthy and prosperous life or whether social segregation defines whether one may enjoy a good education and proper health care. And, one should ask that if something that widely advertised as the benefit of a free market society entertains a rather exclusive circle of beneficiaries who manage to let it appear as a system without an alternative although it inevitably leads to widespread social exclusion. One should, maybe, ask why it can be possible that while productivity is constantly on the rise and per capita income is ever increasing the vast majority of Europeans have to endure that their standard of living is declining. As a journalist I do not wish to engage in any political debate, but I rather like to present facts everyone should know and based on those make up his mind. It is not for me to judge about right or wrong in politics but as an economist I can differ between Minus and Plus, Zero and One, Hausse and Baisse and as a writer I may distinguish between cynicism and humanism and by opening eyes into which main stream media constantly throws sand I may contribute to a lively, democratic and academic debate.

Ralph T. Niemeyer

Berlin, 22nd February 2008

I.

The Best of All Times

4 times in 300 years

✦

Today's Crisis allows for Reminiscence of 1929

Same 'global players'—same scenario, new means

22nd January 2008

"History, in a certain way, does repeat itself. To know about the past helps understand the future" John Kenneth Galbraith wrote in 1988[1]. In an excellent study he explained what had happened in the pretext of 1929, now let's relate his findings to our present crisis:

The well renowned investment house Goldman Sachs in unusual sharp terms warned last week of a recession in the US effecting the world's economy. After August 11th (2007) and in the aftermath of the credit crisis in the US it is indeed not too far fetched to speak of an economic downturn as every granny today knows that the crisis is not over yet. But what most commentators still don't want to say is that it will not only be a recession which many say is "cyclical" and in this way kind of "normal" implying that the market will sort it out by itself but rather a depression of the kind of 1929. The truth is that the markets won't self—regulate and by this manage the crisis. If one analysis the four times capitalism got into severe crisis leading to major wars and even world wars, one can see similar mechanisms leading to the build-up as today.

---

1.   The Great Crash 1929—published 1988 by Houghton Mifflin Company, Boston, USA

Today's crisis started with Clinton & Gore's dot.com bubbles

In a few instances Harvard scholar John Kenneth Galbraith who had been US Ambassador to India during the Kennedy—presidency and since that time is seen as left-leaning fails to keep a neutral perspective. He certainly didn't like Ronald Reagan and although he admits that the double deficit of the Reagan years had only be used by Wall Street as an excuse for the October 1987 crash, but his suggestion that the generous tax relief granted by Reagan for the ultra rich had sparked the crisis is only partly true as it had also been the lowering of the interest rate that had pumped cheap money into the market. In fact, Reagan even rose taxes as he saw that things got out of hand. And, in all fairness, he had been the first president to put significant funds behind Social Security once developed by Harry S. Truman. It had been William J. Clinton who in 1994 limited social security to once a life for 5 years per person. The memory of the electorate, especially if not politically interested may have forgotten about it but the organised voter's instincts might work still and make it hard for Senator Hillary Rodham Clinton to be endorsed outright despite a massive support by media and markets.

So to see Reagan, although often seen by leftist commentators as a hardliner who only was in business with the ultra rich, is not quite correct. And, Reagan's vice president and successor, George Herbert Walker Bush, almost strangled himself when during the 1988 election campaign infamously said "Read my lips: No tax increases." Only to be proven wrong little time later when he was president. In reality, Clinton granted more tax relieves than Reagan and Bush senior did. But, Reaganomics, a pro-cyclic deficit spending to finance a ruinous nuclear arms race to bring the "evil empire" (Reagan about the USSR) down to it's knees had become the trademark of the hardliner's presidency. However, this can hardly been made responsible for the October 1987 crash as it had been rather the lowering of the interest rates that pumped money into the market that had created on leverage basis tools for mega fusions and mergers that had been financed by the sudden influx of cheap money that had followed the high interest rates during the time of the administration of James Carter who tried to fight off inflation in the traditional way. Like in 1929 Goldman Sachs played a major role in the build up of 1987 as the investment bank financed the investment trusts and later "mutual funds" like they did until recently engage in the so called "hedge funds industry" of which the only misleading term is the term "industry". So it is a bit hypocritical for Goldman Sachs to now complain that things again got out of control, the third time since they have become a major player in this theatre.

2008: Once more German capital stands against US capital

Goldman Sachs' chief economist in Frankfurt, Jim O'Neill, this week sees Germany as a winner in the current crisis but that is only partly true as Germany suffers from a shrinking domestic demand due to low wages and a ruined social net as well as high inflation. In fact, Germany only benefits from it's export of capital goods which are (due to the strong Euro) relatively cheaply produced in former Socialist Eastern European states who joined the EU recently. The growth rates the Clinton-Gore administration had celebrated throughout the nineties have to be seen in a different light as well as these could only be achieved by quality adjustments the Bureau of Economic Analysis (BEA) made first in the capital goods sector (meaning that the US' economic statistics pretended that there was economic growth when a washing machine 10 years earlier had 5 programs but in the 1990ies 10 or 15) and later (even more unhealthy) in the real estate field as well. This is referred to as "hedonic pricing", a way of manipulating statistics, the EU Commission under President José Manuel Barroso has partly applied as well as EUROSTAT confirmed to EUreporter last November. Of course, houses built today should have a higher standard than 20 years ago, but to speak of economic growth in this regard is not only far fetched but dangerous as the housing market over-valued, over financed and over-heated but did not keep production in line with this as mortgages taken out by house owners who because of the new evaluation suddenly felt rich were either used for consumption or for buying stocks and shares which further enhanced the bubble building.

1999: Capital withdrawn from production put on casino tables

Now, as payback time has come markets and banks have a hard time to materialise the debt while for millions of American families social existence becomes a privilege leaving the majority ruined. During the whole real estate boom the absolute number of houses had not increased as much as the fake growth rates of the hedonic pricing suggest. At least Germany still produces (and let's produce intermediate products in the Eastern EU member states) goods it exports. The

US instead can only stare at the ruins of the Clintonesque bubble building that had drawn capital out of DOW JONES listed production plants in the nineties and poured it into NASDAQ dotcoms popping up like mushrooms. In 1999 NASDAQ rose by 114% while DOW JONES only grew by 2%. Companies like General Motors or Chrysler closed down major production plants and laid of tens of thousands of employees. Other industries followed as it had become more promising to multiply billions on Wall Street's virtual reality casino tables rather than create economic growth by production. As a result, the US' trade balance along with the triple deficit (Budget, Trade and Performance Deficit, Reagan only had been confronted with a double deficit—budget and trade while the Dollar in a bi-polar world was not rivalled by the Euro) nowadays has become Bush's nightmare for which also war does not pose as a way out anymore.

2008: Green technology—hype just a short sighted exit strategy

After the disastrous collapses of the e-business and dot-com bubbles initiated in the US by Clinton & Gore (the latter who always liked to present himself as the inventor of the internet) and in Europe by Chancellor Gerhard Schröder's *Neuer Markt* which made every granny knock her piggy bank and buy stocks and shares of companies which were not worth the paper their balance sheet was printed on, the bubbles had to find a new playground: this time it was the real estate boom. After the credit crunch of the heavily overvalued real estate market let it collapse the remaining 3000 billion US Dollars are now wobbling into the "green technology" market which already is over-funded anyhow, but again, like in a snowball system the *Green DAX* will not be able to absorb the liquidity completely and accumulate more and more money in double digit profit margins without having a direct impact on production and growth of the real economy. The system works very simple: Nothing needs to be produced, no house needs to be built, just the evaluation and the promise that it will further rise will create the hype. The perversion can be seen in the fact that all analysts and rating agencies are creating—with the help of mainstream media—such a hype that every granny wants to be part of it but once she is in it the big ones pull out. Granny's piggy bank replaces the clients of Goldman Sachs, Merrill Lynch, Salomon Brothers and other *global players*.

Granny on the hook—Goldman Sachs' clients safe in heaven

One could also say that Granny knocked her piggy bank for these institutional investors and Ultra High Net Worth Individuals (UHINWI's) as Merrill Lynch calls them. In Reality, nothing had ever justified the hype as not any tool was used, no additional product being produced and sold, no house being built. It all only happens on paper. And, by applying the so called "hedonic pricing" houses being recently built can due to certain quality adjustments be valued much higher than the market actually would allow for them being sold. Of course, a house built in 1999 has a different standard than a house being built in the seventies of last century. But does the quality adjustment represent a real economic growth? Not unless you wish to lie into your own pocket as a German saying goes.

One could as well tell everyone to buy a sack of cement and sell it on to someone who is more stupid than one selves to pay even more money for it. Once a crowd believes that they will find more and more, even more stupid people than they themselves were, to pay a higher price than they themselves did for a quite useless product, it won't take long until some of them will start to horde sacks of cement in anticipation that this development will go on and on and that they will become ultra rich and that everybody else who didn't understand their happiness was stupid or narrow minded or even an intellectual.

80 years ago exactly the same happened: 1928 was a good year

US President Coolidge on 4th December 1928 noted in front of both houses of Congress that the times were economically almost too good to be true. Record wealth had been accumulated while production and employment in the 1920ies had constantly been on the rise. Although wages stagnated (like we see it since a few years in the EU as well) a certain price stability had been maintained and made it endurable. The latter is out of tune in today's scenario. The "food basket" has been replaced by the "consumption basket" and now contains hundreds of more goods which, like electronics, laptops, digital cameras and laptops, have become relatively cheaper due to "hedonic pricing" (meaning that the EU now follows the sick model of the US be partly applied by allowing quality adjustments indicate that there is economic growth where actually there isn't any). In the 1920ies life has been good to many. Between 1925 and 1929 the amount of producing industries in the US rose by some 19%. At the same time the Florida real estate boom created a speculation—bubble, which we also see today in the US but also in Ireland, Spain, Eastern Europe and Malta where building boom Junkies are making a fortune on the back of tax payers who have to jump in when the bubble bursts. Granny who had trusted the national TV station who said that, yes, there was a good opportunity to increase the personal portfolio which after state has pulled out of funding pensions was small enough, is about to loose it all.

"Everglades" sold to alligators, sand brought to Florida's beaches

In Florida in 1928 it really all looked too good to be true. Like in the 1720ies when John Law's "South Sea" bubbles had ended that speculation and lead to a major financial crisis in Paris, an epoch of economic wealth ended with the greatest to date known financial craziness leaving growth rates part from reality. Like today, already back then those who doubted had been branded as not being on the height of times. In Florida it has been exactly like that. When in 1925 England under Chancellor of the Exchequer, Winston Churchill, had returned to the gold standard and by this let the Pound Sterling, Gold and US Dollar reinstate it's post WWI relation, inflation in Great-Britain hit the ceiling as all export was channelled to the US at a rate of 4.86 US Dollars for one Pound Sterling. British and European gold de-fluxed to the US although prices across the Atlantic were high and interest rates low. Usually, it would be vice versa. The reason for this abnormal 'behaviour' of the capital was simple: the property boom in Florida attracted foreign capital as it promised a tremendous return on investment within as little as 14 days. The only problem was that in most cases land was not sold to build on it but just to be sold on. Even moors and the "Everglades" were not safe from being traded.

Like in 2006 red flags in 1926 had been ignored

The mere expectation of a price rise within days let every crocodile become blind on both eyes and every shark jump out of the sea. What made the whole hype even more attractive was the fact that other than in a normal property transaction where the buyer has to pay the agreed purchasing price for the piece of land he wishes to acquire but is also confronted with obligations as to develop it or make otherwise use of it in order to be entitled to a return on his investment and in this regard is subject to a certain commercial risk, clever bankers and brokers invented a system which separated the transaction as such from the property along with it's obligations to pay for it in full and develop it along with any commercial risk. The trick employed was simple: as in all earnest no development had been envisioned but just the re-selling at a higher price, only pre-sale contracts and options to buy were sold, "the ideal situation for any speculator" John Kenneth Galbraith writes. Theoretically, this would be a financial *prepetuum mobile* which, of course, also in Physics doesn't exist. That it doesn't exist in property or any other booms had been learnt the hard way by those fortune seekers who had come too late: without a related reason and like these things psychologically sometimes kick in, a devastating storm on 28th September 1926 causing the death of some 400 people in Florida, all of a sudden let prices become subject to gravitation laws from Physics. What is so tricky about booming markets which collapse is that not only are warning signs ignored but even when everything goes down the drain, someone collects from underneath the drain those funds which are supposedly lost. In reality, and here Galbraith needs to be corrected, money can not vanish, it just changes ownership. Seen from those speculator's point of view who had come too late and mourns the loss of his skyrocketing profit maximisation dreams, this, of course, does not pose for a comforting explanation. So what did the capital do after it was handed over by the unfortunate speculator to the more powerful and now even richer speculator? It created the next hype, this time a mere stock market boom that culminated in Summer 1927 when even Henry Ford closed down his famous Michigan production plants as he withdrew his funds and put them onto the ever rising stock market. One spoke of *Depression* amid steadily rising stocks and shares while industrial production came to a halt and all wheels stood still.

In our times: real estate boom follows stock market hype

Unlike in the 1920ies in our times we first see the stocks boom and by the injection of cheap money (rather than Reagan's tax policy) by the Federal Reserve create a financial excess which, like in an alcohol excess, later retracts. In 1987 it led to a financial meltdown in October. Excessive alcohol consumption lets the brain shrink. One should think that whoever has endured such would leave his hands from it, but in both scenarios the junkies start all over again after their soar head can differ numbers and bottles again. Clinton and Gore initiated the e-business boom and the honourable and widely respected Fed chairman Alan Greenspan helped fuel the market until he himself lost control of it on 3rd January 2001. He had just decided to lower the interest rate again which led to NASDAQ rise by 14.2% in only one day letting the value of all American stocks skyrocket by some unbelievable 700 billion Dollars. But only one day later everything was back to normal again. And when Greenspan lowered interest rates again by half a per cent each time in February and March 2001 stocks tumbled into a mini-recession and nothing like a phenomenal growth could be stimulated. Greenspan's tools were loosing their power. After September 11th which provided for a market rectification putting the emphasis on the DOW JONES listed military—industrial complex and the oil industry and let NASDAQ shares dwindle ever faster as all signs pointed towards a major war, the next boom was already well on its way: the overvalued—property boom financing consumption and a self-feeding Hausse—once more the myth of a financial perpetuum mobile came up.

Scam artists couldn't do it better: balance act on burst tight rope

The most celebrated innovation in the financial world has been the so called "Asset Backed Securities" (ABS) which are consisting of presumably somehow guaranteed packages of loans. One version of the ABS are the so called "Residential Mortgage Backed Securities" (RMBS). In the latter loans of different risk categories are pooled meaning not only the interest and terms for re-payment of principle are important but also and very much so the potential default rate. The trick the financial institutions employed in order to spread the risk when placing the RMBS on the financial market was simple: they split them into 3 (or, in some cases, more) trenches while each of these trenches are dealing with the potential default in different ways. These provided for the playground of the Hedge Funds whose 'speciality' is lying in obtaining the maximum profit out of risky investments. By the mere construction of the RMBS the wildfire-like creation of virtual funds had not been brought to it's worst yet. The next trick employed was to have 100 of such mortgage-bundles to be bundled into another package, the so called 'Collateralised Debt Obligations' (CDO), which were brought to the market by pretty much the same method. The trick of the double guaranteed and diversified trenches allowed it to transform high-risk loans into a seemingly safe investment. And, because these dubious CDOs appeared to be almost risk free, the demand never eased off and by selling more and more of them allowed banks to issue more high risk loans without really taking on any risk themselves. That really was the license to print money. In the past months and weeks it has become clear that these Standard & Poor's, Moody's and Fitch AAA ratings of the CDOs have been as fraudulently manipulated as the ratings of WORLDCOM, ENRON and Parmalat, who also just until very short before their collapse had received the best ratings. Because the rating agencies are not neutral observers of the scene but earn their money with such manipulations one shouldn't be too surprised about their ruthlessness. At present one bank after the other sees a lot of foam being presented at its cashier's desks and all one knows is that it is not over yet.

EU Commission & EP help build bubbles by MIFID & tax policy

And, by making MIFID become effective last autumn EU Commission and EU council further enhanced the deregulation of the financial markets while this week the European Parliament voted in favour of the Kauppi—report on taxes sending out a clear signal that ongoing competition between member states on income and corporate taxes (while consumer taxes constantly go up) will lead to a tax dumping competition, a spiral that is already pointing downwards and will like in 1929 when Andrew W. Mellon (founder of the Mellon Bank) as Treasury Secretary of the Hoover administration lowered taxes for the rich, further enhance the bubble building. It would be prudent for EU institutions too study the financial history of the 20th century carefully and not run blindfolded into a predictable disaster. The conservative *Frankfurter Allgemeine Zeitung (F.A.Z.)* noted in it's front page editorial on 2nd January 2008 under the headline *"Die Systemfrage"('System-question')* that "some people only now understand how much the competition with Communism as long as it existed, had also tamed Capitalism. Out of itself Democracy and free market economy are not more immune against self destruction than totalitarian systems. In contrast to the latter these do have breaks built in, but these have to be checked and serviced continuously.... in order to sustain our society's vitality. Before others put the *Systemfrage* up, our elites should do it." There is nothing to add.

1927: IOU-bubble, 1987: Bonds for Junkies, 2007: Hedge-fledging

In spring 1927 the Federal Reserve lowered the base rate from 4% to 3.5%, mostly because of pressure from Great-Britain, France and Germany. The "Gold standard" was also given up in order to help European money markets. More and more money backed by neither gold nor production was printed. Treasury bonds were bought by the Fed by bulk as banks and privateers sold and again profited from the cheap influx of cash by the central bank which they directly re-invested in stocks. A fantastic speculation—orgy followed and as usual it were mostly young people who turned the biggest wheels of fusions financed by so called I Owe You (IOU) commercial papers investment trusts like Goldman Sachs or United Founders who through agents created a pyramid of holdings that were 8–10 levels deep and by this let them create empires. What was new at that time was the institutionalising of leverage with innovative tools of small amount of stocks and shares which transformed huge debts into such commercial papers, a method which in 1987 was again presented as a new idea but this time was given a proper name: "Junk Bonds". In 1929 like in 1987 interest rate—fixed obligations replaced traditional securities. In the 1990ies other "tools" to spin a big wheel with a minimal real capital injection were found, so called Derivatives. Until today more and more of these financial instruments are created that prompted ECB President Jean-Claude Trichet at last year's Davos World Economic Forum express his deepest concern about "very sophisticated financial instruments we don't know of" and that the situation should be "observed closely". Frightening to think that our chief financial officer of the EU seems to be drowning in the sea of miss—speculation.

1928—a good year, as nobody dared to ask what was produced

In March 1928 then the average growth rate of emissions had been 25% by providing even for new emissions daily gains of 10–15%. Nobody asked what was actually produced (like during the Clinton-Gore dotcom hype). Major investors, Ultra High Net Worth Individuals (UHINWIs) as Merrill Lynch calls them in it's World Wealth Reports, were pushing the market giving the impression that everyone could become rich without working. The fairy tale from the dish washer who became a millionaire was invented but forgotten the little aspect that most

dish washers stayed in their job for all of their lives as no one gave them the starting capital to participate in the speculation. The fairy tale that every dish washer
could become a millionaire needed to be told. But reality is that most dish washers remain dish washers all their lives through, like in a fairy tale, not everyone
who looks like Cinderella will find her prince.

It was, however, vital to keep up the myth that everyone could and did participate in the boom but in 1928, like today, has been nothing but media brain-
washing otherwise the whole system would have lost acceptance. Of the 120
million people living in the United States of America in 1928 the 29 stock
exchanges counted exactly 1,548,707 clients of which 1,371,920 by profession
were either bankers, traders, brokers or agents themselves and by working for
firms being members of the stock exchanges contributed to the financial incest.
600,000 of these "clients" bought stocks by collaterals and 950,000 paid for it by
cash most of which had been lent to them. Also today, 83% of all stocks in the
US are held by only 5% of society and are mostly inherited. No dish washer ever
got to that point and now even dish washers are automated—like money making.
In Germany, only 8% of the adult population owns stocks. 248 multi billionaires
control 50% of the world's economic output. World population rises slower than
productivity so there shouldn't be poverty at all, but as long as our economic systems allows for speculation that should rather be left to betting offices, this won't
change. On the other hand, the impact miss—speculation has on everybody's
lives is tremendous as we see once more as the real economy heavily suffers under
the present financial turmoil.

The Silence of the Lemmings

Throughout 1928 the Federal Reserve (like Greenspan did it in the 1990ies and
until 2001) helped actively create the bubbles. Treasury Secretary Mellon and
President Coolidge let it simply go. The only one who was sceptical, at least he
says so in his memoirs, has been trade secretary Hoover, however, he managed to
have his scepticism be kept a secret otherwise one would not have during this
election year have thought that the craziness could continue with him even better. The Times Industries Index in only one day rose by 4.5 points as the amount
of traded shares on 12th June 1928 reached a record number of 4,894,670. In all
of 1928 Times rose from 245 to 331 so by 86 points in one year. Radio Index
even more from 85 to 420 although there had never been a dividend being paid
out as—like in NASDAQ in the 1990ies—no such real economic growth had
justified the share prices. DuPont rose from 310 to 525, Montgomery Ward

from 117 to 440, Wright Aeronautic from 69 to 289. In the end one counted 920,550,032 share trading in 1928, whereas it had been 576,990,875 in 1927. This shows that there has been no substance but like in all booms the mere speculation justifies the rises. Income from production, the creation and use of wealth is all dead theory. In November 1928 Hoover has been elected as president in a landslide election as Wall Street had warned that a Congress controlled by Democrats and a president Smith would lead to recession. Not Smith but Hoover had been said to guarantee a continuation of the "good times" with Mellon as treasury secretary. On 7th November 1928, a day after the elections the so called "Victory Boom" let stocks and shares skyrocket by 15% in one day. By 17th November 1928 Times sighted a cyclone-like dynamic. But, just a month after the beginning of "Victory Boom", on 8th December 1928 a first little "irritation" could be noticed as Radio lost 72 points in only one day. Like today, 'analysts' also and foremost those of Goldman Sachs, were quick to say that this was just a normal and small disturbance that could always occur. And, for a moment it looked as if they had been right as overseas one realised that in New York one could get money for 5% as the Fed had lowered the interest rate to 3.5% but if one could buy stocks and use such as collateral to buy more stocks bearing at least some 12% profit share, all on credit basis, so a massive gold stream headed to Wall Street from around the globe to participate in the *Arbitrage* deal. This led to producing companies decide not to produce goods anymore but withdraw funds from production and just let it multiply on the market. All this can be observed nowadays at an even larger scale as well. The latest news suggest that NOKIA is about to close down a profitable production plant in Bochum, Germany.

In 1929 "I don't like Mondays"—could have been a hit as well

On 4th December 1928 Goldman Sachs and Company created the Goldman Sachs Trading Corp. that operated as an Investment Trust. Until September 1929 this Investment Trust house sold investment papers for 600 million Dollars each month having gained in less than 3 months more than 300% in value. On 20th August 1929 'Blue Ridge' another investment house and many others followed throughout every day in August and September of 1929. Years later a Senate investigative committee interrogated Mr. Sachs who had to admit that his company had sold overvalued shares at a rate of 104 which at the time he was questioned only had a value of 1.75 US Dollars. Most of the stocks traded at that time had been such of well known industries such as American Telephone and

Telegraph Company, Allied Chemical and Dye, Santa Fe, Eastman Kodak, General Electric, Standard Oil of New Jersey and many more. The only problem was, that the inflated prices of those stocks and shares never reflected the real economic growth. Like later in 1987 (the Investment Trusts now were called "Mutual Funds" and today "Hedge Funds") and today in January 2008 (as the US reports the worst inflation rate in 17 years) this led to a devaluation of prices and wages, a logic consequence of economic excess which, again, like after excessive alcoholic consumption causes retraction. The brain shrinks.

On Monday, 21st October 1929 more than 6 million stocks were sold in only one day. An unprecedented record number. On Thursday, 24th October 1929, 12,894,650 stocks were up for sale, but there were no buyers anymore.

Kaputtalism: only way out is war

The tragedy is, and that should raise the fundamental question as to why the whole Investment Trust—, Mutual—or Hedge Funds—"industry" is still legal, that in 1928 and still in 1929 the capacity of the producing industries had, in relation to the available real income actually justified expansion and would have triggered a sustainable growth as the productive capacity of the industries perfectly matched consumer spending, demand and purchasing power, an rather ideal situation which evidently was destroyed by the *un*real creation of speculation bubbles. A recession or depression has been absolutely unnecessary and all theorists who say that this is a normal cycle only say so because they are bribed by the system. We are in exactly the same situation today. In the UK, chancellor of the Exchequer, Darling, noted in October 2007 that the *real* economy was in good shape. That is true. The only question is why are we like in 1720, 1929, 1987 and nowadays allowing speculators to rule over our industries and by this over us?

Each time Capitalism is in crisis it destroys all values, financial ones, production lines, even moral values. Millions and Billions of people are feeling the impact in one way or the other. The dish washer who never made it to become a millionaire hears the elite mourn the millions and billions that supposedly had gone down the drain although this is not quite correct as someone underneath the sink has opened the pipe and redirects those funds thought to have gone down the drain back into the next bubble. In the aftermath of the crisis in 1929 President Hoover opened all taps and offered tax relief while Rockefeller bought shares by bulk, thus bringing back some confidence. This has of course not been a selfless act but a well calculated one as he made a fortune even in the greatest crisis of modern times. This will be like that now, 80 years later as well. And, like back then, the ordinary citizen will be told through mainstream media that markets are recovering and all will be fine again, just these unfortunate war times one has to get over and the citizen should rather not rock the apple cart but defend the country and it's values because if the economy is doing well, everyone will feel it, they usually say. History, we are taught these days once more repeats itself, but by some extra pirouettes of which the last dance will be danced backwards.

As surprising as the burning of the Reichstag

75 years ago, Adolf Hitler, although he had never won a majority in any elections (in July 1932 it had been some 37% for his NSDAP, in the next elections in November of the same year it had already been a sharp decline by 8% leaving the NAZI-party financially almost ruined and demoralised as members de-fluxed to other parties) all of a sudden was supported by banks and leading industrialists of the 'Düsseldorf Club' such as steal magnate Krupp and the Quandt family (who benefited tremendously from slave labour in the concentration camps and today build BMWs). Even today these circles have a say in throwing in the German's upper class support for a candidate for the chancellorship. One of the bankers, Kurt von Schröder, who organised a meeting on 4th January 1933 in his house in Köln with centrist former Reichschancellor Franz von Papen who by supporting Hitler saw a chance for a comeback for himself after he had been outmanoeuvred by Reichspresident von Hindenburg and his former friend, the present Reichschancellor Schleicher who only stayed in office for 57 days, had been among those who had been heavily benefiting from the aftermath of 1929 and had become one of the heavyweights of Germany's banking scene which together with the heavy industry and their shareholders must have seen a possibility for an economic recovery for Germany when playing the nationalistic card rather than being further dragged into the financial turmoil of the rest of the world. "Globalisation" although not called like that in those days was sealed to be over in that night.

1933: A little bit of Myths—busting

It is always said that the depression of 1929 had created an ungovernable situation in Germany in the 1930ies which is partly correct. But, the German stock market in Frankfurt am Main had left it's worst times behind and already closed

30 points higher again while unemployment had dropped by one million in January 1933. Chancellor Schleicher just had issued a 500 million Reichsmark public employment program but the fruits of his idea were already credited to the new choice of Germany's elite, the WWI private and freshly baked Reichschancellor Adolf Hitler who in a coup d'état after his SA brigades had planted an arson attack on the Reichstag building on 27th February 1933 quit the alliance with Franz von Papen's Centrists and then could take the whole power with all the horrific consequences we know today from history books. It can be worthwhile not only to read the political and military history of the 20th century but also about it's financial history.

Someone sucks

◆

New German chic: Manager bashing

Christmas 2007

It has become fashionable these days in Germany to cite the great disparity in the standard of living between bottom and top of society. Deutsche Bank AG chairman Josef Ackermann must have fallen from his sofa as Mrs. Merkel all of a sudden accused the German managers of filling their pockets. Mr. Ackermann must have felt treated unfairly as his 13 million Euros per year had never been seen as exorbitant in international comparison. Porsche AG's Mr. Wiedekind's 70 million Euros pay after he managed to take over VW (with the help of the EU commission) also look modest in comparison to what managers in the US earn. And, hasn't it been the politicians who have made it possible that more money remained in the pockets of Germany's top management elite by lowering the income tax from 53% (during Helmut Kohl's chancellorship) to 42% (after Schröder's tax reform) while Angela Merkel's CDU-SPD coalition just decided to introduce a flat tax on capital income of 25% replacing the 42% personal income tax for the ultra rich receivers of interest from 2009 on? Germany's shareholders also must rub their eyes as same Chancellor Angela Merkel has further lowered the corporate tax while VAT and other indirect taxes are going up now mourns the loss of sensibility among managers. It's the hour of the populists.

German *Aufschwung* chokes

After all opinion polls showed an ever greater disappointment of the vast majority of Germans with their economic system even main stream media does not try to cover up any more that something is wrong as their own credibility would be at stake. 72% of Germans say that the *Aufschwung* (up-swing) Angela Merkel's grand coalition of Christian Democratic Union and Social Democrats were celebrating throughout 2007 is bypassing them. Severe child poverty, a study by *Kinderhilfswerk* found is widespread. German TV channels, worried about their viewing rates, suddenly report on children from families who were thrown into poverty by the labour market reforms infamously called "Hartz IV" referring to the former VW manager Professor Peter Hartz who bribed unionists in order to win support for unfavourable pay-deals he and Social Democratic Chancellor Gerhard Schröder made a dogma of the new German deal *Agenda 2010*. And, another study of *Deutsches Institut für Wirtschaft*, published by DER SPIEGEL found that the disparity in income has never been greater since WWII while more than half of the population own nothing, no car, no house, apartment, maybe a washing machine, and save nothing. The only reason why the German savings rate still slightly increases is to be seen in the fact that the privatisation of the pension system requires to put a little money aside each month. German domestic demand is constantly on the decline (-7.6% volume in retail trade) as wages in 2007 again shrank significantly as even the German tabloid *Bild Zeitung*, usually a rather conservative opinion-guide, noted. New jobs, Mrs. Merkel said she had created, are mostly low paid and bear only a minimum of social security as these are replacing (another idea of Schröder) existing labour relationships which traditionally were governed by a tariff scheme negotiated between employers and unions. Less than 60% of jobs are currently regulated by tariffs. It used to be more than 75%—before Schröder & Merkel.

History teaches: High Inflation & Unemployment means war!

Moreover, a record high inflation eats into household spending. As the consumption basket nowadays contains electronic goods which are said to have become relatively cheaper (although EUreporter discovered recently that quality adjustments, so called "hedonic pricing", only let digital cameras, laptop computers and washing machines appear cheaper) while the prices for basic goods, food, fresh fruits and vegetables especially have skyrocketed, an official inflation rate of 2.8% across the Euro-zone mocks the reality Europeans who go on a shopping spree find in the shops. Inflation in the food sector is rather at 25% and hits lower income—or poor families worse. Energy costs have hit the ceiling and it is rather the privatisations in this field and not the high oil price. Since 2000 energy in Germany has become 50% more expensive while shareholder's value rises by some 37% in 2007 alone. Instead of investing into sustainability and safer networks, costs for the consumer as well as profit shares increase simultaneously. The times have gone when main stream media lent their microphones to politicians who maintain that everything is under control.

German expansion—crisis

So where has the German *Aufschwung* gone? If Germans are not consuming anymore as before, how can there be an upswing? With the strong Euro, one would think, the export leaning German economy is vulnerable, isn't it? It is not. Whereas France is suffering heavily and accumulated a 34 billion Euro trade deficit in 2007, Germany can celebrate a record surplus of nearly 100 billion Euros. This is because German industries predominantly produce capital goods such as high technology and cars which are not that easily rivalled whereas France has a hard time to sell it's consumer goods. And, Germany is benefiting from EU's Eastern expansion in two ways: first of all, most of the retailers in the former socialist states are today German, only a few French and British, and secondly, German industries managed well to open production lines in the new member states lowering their wage costs per piece. The strong Euro let's such production become even cheaper. Eastern Europeans now produce intermediate products for German industries. Their own industrial production meanwhile declines as the Western European (mostly German) shopping malls carry top shelf products from the West thus leading to an artificial growth rate and unhealthy trade deficit all Eastern European states who joined in 2004 and 2007 suffer from. Again, France and other Western European economies are staying well behind Germany. The tragedy is that although Germany could do well, it doesn't. To blame Germany's elite is fashionable but short-sighted. What appears to be symptomatic in the German economic system is the alliance of mainstream media with interests of shareholders and owners when it comes to privatisations or the lucrative sale of state assets. Logic, media is owned by owners, conglomerates are controlled by shareholders who usually also have interests in other fields of business or at least have friends who have such. Just the mix between politics and media conglomerates has yet not reached such extravagant heights as in Italy where Former Ex Prime Minister Berlusconi once more getting into the driver's seat after he ate another TV station. And even in France the flirt with the media has ended for President Sarkozy who all of a sudden seems to hate the limelight when it comes to scrutinising his ability of sober judgement of what is suitable for a president of *La Grande Nation* and what would rather belong to Hollywood.

German media these days focuses on tax evasion by prominent top managers and launched the wave by out-casting the CEO of Deutsche Post AG, a state-holding subject to continuing privatisation attempts. Klaus Zumwinkel probably always felt safe relying on a un-outspoken silent agreement between the German media and the owners and shareholders of industries not to attack the German management elite for alleged tax evasions. It must have come as a real shock for Deutsche Post chairman Zumwinkel that on Valentine's Day special fiscal investigators searched his home and office while TV cameras having waited in front of the private residence of Zumwinkel in Köln (Cologne) celebrated the prominent case as the beginning of a witch hunt against all high profile tax evaders. No word about what really had been behind the sudden change of mood of investigators and mainstream media to all of a sudden publicly slaughter icons of free market fetishisms. A few days later, on 18ᵗʰ February 2008, readers of the daily *Handelsblatt*, could read under the front-page headline "Berlin now prepares sale of Postbank, that "bankers and federal government officials were eager to de-regulate the German banking industry further" and that "Postbank played a central role in the scenario although Mr. Zumwinkel was objecting the planned sale and actively threw in his fierce resistance." The conservative *Handelsblatt* concluded that "Mr. Zumwinkel has not made friends with his stance as Postbank was seen as a highly profitable branch of Deutsche Post AG compensating losses from the US express mail business." And, finally after selling Postbank to Commerzbank AG or Deutsche Bank AG, a "shareholders will earn a lucrative special dividend" *Handelsblatt* wrote. In a way, Mr. Zumwinkel who had tried to protect the interests of the public by hindering the sale of Postbank, one of the state's most profitable assets (the only reason why private investors would be interested in buying such), will not receive any bonus but will see his public image permanently be destroyed by his tax affair which he had admitted had been a mistake. He might feel treated unfairly by public opinion leaders, like Ex Bundesbank President Welteke who during the Schröder-government had resisted the sale of the central bank's gold reserves to cover the budget deficit of the Social-Democratic—Green government. Mr. Welteke resigned after a witch hunt by German media who slaughtered him over the fact that he, as a state official, had accepted the invitation for a New Year's dinner and overnight stay in Berlin's famous Adlon Hotel by a Commerzbank AG board member. Needless to say that although the fact that in many other cases this rather common practice had always been tolerated, just illustrated how much business and public interests are widely accepted to be interwoven. The public outcry by Germany's top politicians who, once retiring from a public office find nothing wrong in joining the board of a private enterprise, becomes hollow and in a way hypocritical as most careers are only starting once Ministers but also former chancellor Gerhard Schröder left office.

Who is the worker?

✦

One continent—two worlds

Social Protection in the EU, an unbalanced equation: expenditure-share in GDP declines while productivity rises and purchasing power declines. 72 Million (15%) of citizens live in poverty with further 36% being in acute danger to fall as well. Number of "Working-Poor" rises sharply. 'Per Capita' EU constantly becomes richer, so what is wrong? Let's have first a look at how the EU's economic powerhouse is doing:

October-November 2007

As Germany by it's sheer economic power is setting the tone and also the standard in the EU, it is worthwhile to have a closer look at how the Euro-zone's biggest economy is handling it's affairs. Sooner or later this will have effects on the rest of the EU anyhow. In many countries the German model is copied already. Germany is admired by many for it's effectiveness, accurateness and efficiency, and for it's accumulation of wealth. In poorer regions of Europe one might envy the Germans. German export is rising to all time highs, overtaking France by bulk (German trade surplus in 2007 is already 94 billion Euros, France's trade deficit at 27 billion as of October), putting the UK and Italy into the shadow as well. So the German *Aufschwung* (up-swing) is picking up speed, one would think, but how do the ordinary citizens benefit from it? Domestic demand is collapsing (-7.6% of volume in retail trade in the first three quarters of 2007). On the other hand, one hears of Germany being the richest country in the EU. Germans are as rich as never before.[1] Per Capita the Germans become richer and richer. By the end of 2006, the monetary accumulation reached some 4.53 trillion Euros, 240 billion more than in 2005. The private capital sector grew by 6% although the growth rates tumbled below 2%. Most of the newly accumulated

---

1. SPIEGEL online 09th January 2007

wealth (4/5) stems from the rises in the DAX listed stocks which grew by some unreal 22%.

Savings rate would decline rapidly if it was not for private pension schemes

The saving's rate, instead declined rapidly, it is lower now than it has been in 2005. People are de-saving rather than saving. It would even decline faster if the public pension system was not "modernised" by replacing state transfers with private pension funds. So they are spending money but at the same time the domestic demand is declining by already some 7.4% in volume of retail trade in the first 9 months of 2007. Doesn't that sound like a contradiction? Where is all the money gone? This is only explicable when one scrutinises who earns all these wonderfully multiplied investments? To say that Germans per capita become richer and richer does not mean that every "capita" becomes richer. Only less than 10% of Germans own stocks while 70% of all stocks are held by the top 1% of society. This week, DER SPIEGEL magazine[2] quoted from a study published by the reputable economic science institute *Deutsches Institut für Wirtschaftsforschung* (DIW). In it's detailed analysis the institute finds that 10% of the population own and control two thirds of all German wealth[3] which today is 5.4 trillion Euros, while more than half of the population have almost nothing they own. The total income of the latter is used up for consumption or for retiring loans. And, there is still a growing gap between East and West Germans. According to the DIW study West Germans own 2.6 times more than East Germans illustrating who had won and who had lost the cold war. This has also to do with the disparity of income: East Germans are still being paid lower wages than West Germans although the costs in both parts of Germany are increasingly levelling out. "Because of the higher income of the richest citizens the social unbalances have become bigger" the study finds. The wage share in the total wealth since 1996 is stagnating whereas the capital share on total wealth has risen by 4% to 33.8%. The upper class is consuming their easily earned money as it is reflected in the sharp increase of demand for luxury goods. At the same time, the discount retailers report growing market shares. The gap between rich and poor in the

---

2.   06th November 2007 SPIEGEL online

3.   including property, yachts, cars, cash deposits, stocks, shares, life insurances and pensions, antiques, arts, jewellery, numismatic coins and stamps. The debts are already separated from the total wealth figure.

Euro-zone's powerhouse becomes a gulf. Nevertheless, Economic and Monetary Affairs Commissioner Joaquin Almunia speak about "economic good times" in Germany. For many citizens this comes along as a cynical joke as the most prominent lie of the "Ideo*un*logists" and neo-liberal hardliners is combined with demographics.

What neo-liberal columnists and politicians are never getting tired to describe is the fact that the demographic pyramid of an ever faster aging population inevitably leads to one working person to carry 1.6 persons on her/his shoulders in the year 2050 while in 2000 it has been 1 worker, entrepreneur or employee to provide for 1.1 other person, each. The neo-liberal ideologists try to tell us that because until the seventies of last century 2 working people were catering for one pensioner whereas it will be vice versa in the very near future, there would not be enough wealth for distribution to maintain the standard of living for all. Therefore, they say, one should invest into private pension schemes. They fail, of course, to give us a valid reason why a private company would be better in maintaining the standard of living for all of us than the state. Apart from the usual nonsense that state controlled pension funds would be less efficient than private ones (for which there has been no examples yet, but indeed for private pension funds going bankrupt in each and every financial crisis) there is nothing bearing any logic that would support their argument. This may have to do with the fact that the underlying ideology of the demographic pyramid that supposedly will be turned from bottom to top and for that reason not be sufficient anymore is already false. Not only is it not true that because of an decreasing population figure while we are all living ever longer there wouldn't be a big enough cake to feed us all when we are old, but it is a simple to dismantle lie. The logic applied shall suggest that every working person will have to feed ever more people and should not wonder if there would be less and less for himself and those depending on him. What usually is being forgotten is the fact that the dependencies in 1975 have also been greater in 1975 because more children had been born until then. The relation of those times will only be outnumbered in the year 2022, but even if that happens, one should not worry too much. The simplifying relation "pensioner-employee" shall illustrate that our system is unhealthy and unsustainable. The story of the starving baker who has to share his pie with ever more unproductive eaters is a myth based on two completely illogic assumptions: Firstly, it is assumed that the pie the baker is baking and selling won't become bigger but for the next 50 years will stay the same. Secondly, one assumes that the amount of bakers in the various years to come will remain the same. Neither the first, nor the second assumption is founded in any logic and historic experience. The only valid logic statistical measurement which defines the size of the pie baked per baker is the *productivity*. Productivity rose in Germany since 1960 by some 2.5% annually. Even if we assumed that this growth shrank to only 1% per annum the population in 50 years—every eater, young and old—would still be able to eat a piece of the pie which will be 12% larger than today. If productivity increased as an average by 2% annually it would even be a piece of cake that is increased by a third. And, this would even be the case if unemployment remained as high as it is today. If, for instance, more people were given the opportunity to participate in pie-baking, these figures would look even better. Therefore, the statement that the state backed pension system became obsolete because of the so called "demographic factor" is a simple lie. A lie employed by those who advocate private pension funds as if there were bigger pieces of the pie available for everyone in a system in which everyone was only caring for himself than in the state-run solidarity system. If the demographic pension lie was only partly true it would hit the private, capital-backed pension funds in exactly the same way. The standard of living of the pensioners always has to be covered by the current GDP and nothing else. The generation being in the production process has to work for what the elder generation wants to consume, be it privately administrated pensions or state backed pensions. Nobody wants to eat bonds or coupons when being old, but everyone wants to eat bred, fish, meat, drink good wine, wear warm clothes, visit nice restaurants, travel the world. If such services aren't provided for in sufficient numbers, the nicest private pension insurance policy will only be an inflationary piece of paper and ultimately be worth nothing. In other words: it is not about demographics but interests. Privatisations always have beneficiaries, also the privatisation of the pension schemes:

1. the class of higher income who by excluding the solidarity principle only provide flower and baking powder for their own pie;

2. the corporations in general as these can reduce labour costs; and

3. insurance and financial conglomerates who can use the flower and baking powder for creating speculation bubbles which, if it goes well, may result in a mega cake.

Unfortunately, the latter usually does not go well over a longer period, at least not a period long enough to create sustainability for a decent pension system, and results in these private schemes in the end becoming reliant on the state again, the one the advocates of the privatised pension scheme are said to hate so much. In the end the rich always rely on the solidarity of the working class who produces the goods they wish to consume.

Disillusioned Youth: Children in richest EU country in Poverty trap

The German Spiegel magazine reports that children in Germany, presumably the richest EU member, are born into poverty.[4] 17% of the 8 year old kids see their future negative because they don't find security at home since their parents are unemployed according to a study by World Vision. Children from the lower social classes also see less chance for themselves in the society. The study also shows that young people with a family background of unemployment only seek lower educational levels and see themselves as being disadvantaged for the rest of their lives. The study concludes that there is a wide gap between children of families which aren't well off and those who want for nothing. Since the Social Democratic—Green government of Chancellor Gerhard Schröder went with the chainsaw through the social net of the once balanced German cushioned capitalism while granting tax relief to the multinational corporation and the rich upper class in Germany, a sharp contrast between rich and poor could be noticed. Schröder and the mainstream media cited exploding social costs which were no longer sustainable. The truth was different: The social expenditure in 1975 was 34% of the GNP, in 1994 it was 33.3% and in 1997 slightly higher at 34.4%. No explosion of costs was seen but it is easy to apply to people's greed especially of those who consider themselves middle class and are working hard but have to pay high taxes. President Nicolas Sarkozy of France won the elections by applying to the same greedy instinct of the working middle class of French citizens who also pay high taxes and social contributions while the major corporations are legally reducing their tax obligations and by this force the state to increase the indirect taxes such as VAT and 'ecological' taxes for energy.

The Myths of the 'Modernizers': Liberalise until it comes out of your ears!

Another credo of Schröder but today also of Chancellor Angela Merkel to fight unemployment is to force employees and workers to become more "flexible". EU

---

4.   SPIEGEL online 24th October 2007

Commissioner Spidla invented the so called "Flexicurity" program which is also a much celebrated part of the Lisbon strategy of Stability & Growth. Like the German model it is aimed at replacing labour governed by tariff contracts once negotiated between the unions in all EU states and employer's associations by a "flexible" workforce. In other words: the recruitment agencies are increasing their share in the labour market by leasing out qualified workers to the same companies who once used to employ a person granting a series of social benefits and protection. In Germany it is now less than 60% of protected working relations, down from 72% in 1996, in the East it is less than 40%. It was constantly declining since 1996[5] thus not adding to more security in the labour market. And, new jobs in Germany were only been created by small and medium sized companies (+ 5.6% between 1996 and 2002) while the major corporations in the same time period reduced their workforce by 16.8% according to Financial Times Deutschland[6]. This trend became stronger over the past five years and especially this year in 2007 with the former state-owned service providers Deutsche Telekom laying off 121,000 employees, Deutsche Post 90,000 and Deutsche Bahn 150,000 who became *Aktiengesellschaften* (AG's) and soon will be DAX listed. The further 'liberalisation' of the postal services as demanded by the EU Commission ill costs another 30,000 jobs in the postal sector while TNT and PIN Group are ready to take over the letter delivery—monopoly which in Germany is a nice pie of 10 billion Euros annually. The new monopolists delivering letters to German households like the good old Deutsche Post once did will pay it's employees 40% less and than the postal workers in the state owned company earned until now. Deutsche Post AG pays 11.84 € per hour. TNT will only pay 7 € in West Germany and 5.90 € in the East. Social benefits are also brought down to a minimum. Of the 40 million potentially active workforce of Germany only 24 Million are now holding down a job which bares social benefits and some protection. The jobs growth Angela Merkel celebrated this year is happening only in the lower paid sector of the industries or recruitment agencies. In many cases one could observe a so called "revolving door" effect meaning that employees who used to work in a well paid position in a major company like BMW are laid off only to find themselves working for the same company again, but being indirectly employed through a recruitment agency. The social contributions the employer has to be are much lower as also the benefits are significantly reduced. Of the 1 million new jobs Mrs Merkel's government was overseeing being created

5.   Handelsblatt 13th December 2001
6.   FTD 6th September 2002

this year, 800,000 were with these agencies. This also has an effect on the social benefit scheme which is now chronically under-funded by some 10 billion Euros.

Rhetoric question: "Who is the worker?"

For 2050 projections show that only 24 million people in Germany will work. Of a 82 million population this is a shrinking minority. The rhetoric question once posed by Lenin „Who is the worker?" should be asked again. A new definition of work and production is needed. One has to think about re-distribution of work as well as a fair distribution of wealth in order to level out these changes and have a society which includes and not excludes it's citizens. One should be happy about a constantly rising productivity. In the past 25 years productivity rose by more than 45% (in Germany) so theoretically this would mean today's workers and employees could work 45% less or have 45% more in his pocket than the workers and employees in 1982 had. The reality is the opposite: Clear of inflation the purchasing power today is less than in 1982. The standard of living is continuously declining. At the same time contribution of taxes paid on wages in the total tax income has doubled while the share of corporate taxes has dwindled down to half of what it has been back then. That's why ordinary people are holding back with investing into new cars, household items and also do not save anymore.

Germany—the model for the rest of the EU?

At present, there are less than 4 million unemployed in Germany. Well, one simply pushed long-term unemployed into 1 € an hours jobs, meaning they are paid one € per hour in addition to the social benefits, by this further putting the primary labour market under pressure. Every second company employing workers under the 1€- per hour—scheme admit to use the employee also for regular and not only additional work. In other words: these low paid and non-secured jobs are increasingly replacing the existing primary work relationships. It is also revealed that 29% of these 1-€-an hour jobbers in West Germany and 71% in East Germany do have professional qualifications.

The spiral is pointing downwards as qualified employees are now forced to accept ever lower wages and less social benefits. In 2006 the low paid jobs in Germany exceeded the EU average of 15.1% by hitting the ceiling with 22%.[7] These

---

7.   low paid job is defined as less than two thirds of the median wage level

low paid jobs are drastically on the increase since the government of Gerhard Schröder introduced the so called "Mini-Jobs" in 2003. In 2006 more than 6.7 million people were working under these conditions. The vast majority of them (75%) have a completed professional education, 10% of them even holding an academic degree.[8] Between 1991 and 2005 the amount of part time employees increased from 5.5 million to 11.1 million. In the same time period the amount of fully employed persons decreased from 29.6 to 23.3 million. The average wages are quite competitive within the EU. Germany is only in the middle field of the EU 15 and well below other major economies in Europe. The wage-costs per piece have constantly declined as well. In 2004 by—0.5%, in 2005 by 0.9% and in 2006 by—1.1% so one can really not say that production in Germany is too expensive. In 2007 the low paid sector has increased to now 7 million. Some people are working fro 1.92 € per hour in the cleaning business for five star hotels and offices.[9] A law against such exploitation has never been brought in because the German government doesn't want to "interfere with the tariff autonomy" of the industries as that could lead to unemployment, Mrs. Merkel insists. In other EU countries this has never been an obstacle. The introduction of a minimum wage (in 1999) in the UK has lead to more employment, not less. It is today 5.35 Pounds (8 €). Unemployment was reduced by 5% since 1999. In 18 of 27 EU countries minimum wages are at least law. In Luxembourg the minimum wage is fixed at 9.08€, in Ireland 8.85€, France 8.27€, The Netherlands 8.13€, Czech Republic 1.76€ and Bulgaria 0.53€.

This will increase dramatically although the EU Commission is eager not to report on this anymore as the poverty statistics have bee sacrificed over the Lisbon strategy against poverty which can only be seen as a cynical joke at this stage

Chancellor Merkel's dream of an up-swing

On the other hand, the 30 DAX listed corporations in Germany in 2006 laid off 43,000 employees while Deutsche Telekom plans to outsource some 60,000 of their workforce in order to increase the profit by reducing costs. The same with insurers like Allianz AG, pharmaceutical companies like Bayer AG or defence- and airlines giant Airbus who all also plan to replace employees with more "flexible" and cheaper workforce. All this in the middle of what Mrs. Merkel says is an economic *Aufschwung* (up-swing).

---

8.   Böckler Impuls 5/2006
9.   Der Spiegel 03/2007

Even the conservative German economic daily *Handelsblatt*[10] noted that the "reduction of the social transfers let's cheap discounters grow while traditional retailers are pushed out of the market. On the other hand, luxury goods are booming as well." The explanation for this can be found in the first ever and so far last German government's "poverty report" of 2004 according to which the amount of poor people in Germany has grown between 1998 and 2003 from 12 to 13.5%[11] with another sharp increase after the *Agenda 2010* containing the infamous labour market reform known as "Hartz IV" of Chancellor Gerhard Schröder has picked up momentum. According to the study, child poverty has doubled between 1989 and 2001. Of the 15 million children in Germany every sixth was living below the poverty line and this figure has now sharply increased in the past 2 years as did also the amount of households being desperately over-indebted. Like in the UK, this figure has doubled in those 5 years. So far, the German government was not eager to have a follow-up study on poverty being conducted. But, one may find an indication where the development is leading when one sees that the amount of people who have less than 50% of the average income in Germany between 1999 and 2005 has increased from 12% to 17.4% leaving 25% of East Germans and 4% of West Germans, in total 6.5 million people (8%) feeling "socially excluded"[12] having less than 424 € per household for living while social allowance for unemployed people calculates 3.33 € per day for food per person.

Not only wealth is inheritable—children become a poverty risk

49% of the poor of Germany are stemming from families which already were poor. 83% of children of academics study in a university, but only 23% of children growing up in working class families. Obviously one can not only inherit wealth. Most of these people are also not participating in the democratic process anymore as they say in the study of the Friedrich-Ebert-Stiftung, a foundation financed by former Chancellor Gerhard Schröder's Social Democratic Party (SPD), do not vote at all anymore.

---

10. HANDELSBLATT 17th September 2004
11. Süddeutsche Zeitung (SZ) 23rd December 2004
12. SPIEGEL online 18th October 2006

And, across the EU it is 72 million people (15%) who live under the poverty line with another 36 million being in concrete danger to fall under the same 60%-less-than-medium-income—barrier.

This will increase dramatically although the EU Commission is eager not to report on this anymore as the poverty statistics have bee sacrificed over the Lisbon strategy against poverty which can only be seen as a cynical joke at this stage.

EU Commission fights poverty only by manipulating statistics

In the EU Commission's statistics the disparity in income doesn't look that severe simply because a trick is employed: one does not take the medium but the *median* figures meaning that the top quintile and the bottom quintile are left out of the perspective. So the median income level looks quite good, the incredible accumulation of wealth on the top is not shown while the most dramatic poverty is eradicated, at least by the means of statistics.

Eurostat writes that "preliminary estimates for 2005 show a decline in the share of social protection expenditure in GDP"[13] and that is even worse as in real terms it means that less and less is spent on at least maintaining living conditions and welfare but with a ageing population it means that the elderly especially see their pensions shrink as the purchasing power is constantly declining. Pharmaceutical products have shown steep increases and because of cuts in health care the standard of living is declining further. In Germany, the age pyramid is turned from bottom to top. Therefore, Germany's share of social expenditure in GDP should be above the average of the EU 15, but it is less. On the contrary, France is still well above the average although the population is younger as more children are born. The popular argument is that because of the demographics the social expenditure had exploded and was not sustainable anymore. This is definitely not true as Eurostat proves. In 1975 total expenditure of GDP was 30.7% in Germany, in 2005 it has been 31%. On the other hand, one could very well finance a higher standard of living for pensioners, but also for unemployed and poor people as well as youngsters and also finance education for our youngsters irrespective which class of society their parents belong to since productivity rises steadily and—as Joaquin Almunia, the EU Commissioner or Economic and Monetary Affairs never gets tired to remind us has gone up from 1.2% to 1.5% in the last twelve months. Productivity grows much faster than the population, so where is

---

13.   Eurostat publication 99/2007

the problem to finance a life in dignity for all citizens? Theoretically, we, all 457 million citizens of the EU, per capita become richer and richer, whether a *capita* is eight, eighteen or eighty years old. It is a mere question of distribution of wealth as usual and it should also be in the interest of the rich to level out the huge unbalances in our society because a society in which only the shareholder value counts and children become a poverty risk does not reproduce itself. It becomes cold and lonely.

The Master of the Manipulated Figures

◆

EU Economic Commissioner Almunia's 'Creative' accounting

November 2007

The economic forecast for 2007–2009 presented by Economic & Currency Affairs Commissioner Joaquin Almunia is a bit overshadowed by the high oil price and the August 11—financial turmoil. He expects the growth in the European Union to decelerate from 2.9% in 2007 to 2.4% in 2008 and 2009. This may sound realistic but it is rather not the high oil prices or the financial bubbles that have the biggest impact on the slowdown, it is rather structural problems in the EU. The only growth one finds in all new member states are either in volume of retail trade, meaning that citizens in the east enjoy the West-European top-shelf products, or in construction. New roads are built, houses, apartments, schools, hospitals, all fine, the only problem is that the banks, like in Ireland, Spain and other countries where they had initiated building booms years ago which are now all collapsing, over-finance development and by this let inflation rise. Higher inflation can only be fought off by higher interest rates. Higher interest rates make the financing of the property boom become unsustainable. At the same time as the volume of retail trade[1] sales index gained quite modestly by 1.6% in the Euro-zone, between September 2006 and September 2007, it sky-rocketed in the EU 27 to 3.5%, with the largest increases been observed in Latvia (+17.5%), Poland (+13.3%), Lithuania (+12.7%) and Sweden (+9.8%). Germany, after a long period of negative figures, gained with some 2.3%, a sign of a modest recovery after domestic demand had almost collapsed. The largest

---

1.   Eurostat publication 151/2007 6th November 2007

increases in the sectors of total volume of retail trade are in the foods, drinks, tobacco—sectors, so good to know that the consumption is still up.

Almunia: "Not a good sign if new Euro participant has highest inflation"

The only problem is that the Eastern European member states since 2004 have seen a decline in agricultural and industrial production. All Eastern countries today have negative trade balances after they joined in 2004. Before, they enjoyed a somewhat balanced trade with the EU. Latest figures fro 2007 show the largest surplus to be accounted for by Germany (+114.9 billion €)[2], followed by the Netherlands (+23.6 billion €). The largest deficit was observed in the UK (-78.1 billion €) followed by Spain (-53.3 billion €), France (-22.9 billion €), Romania (-11.6 billion €) and Portugal (-10.1 billion €).

Even Commissioner Almunia seems to be worried: "It is not a good sign that Slovenia as the first one of the new member states to join the Euro in January of this year is threatened by 3% inflation." The inflation is maybe less of a problem in the case of Slovenia compared to the much more severe problem that it's share in total GDP growth of the EU is down from 2% (before joining the Euro) to now some un-erotic 0%. This is really not an enticing prospect for other aspirants of the EU's noble club.

The hedonic pricing—coup: how to manipulate your balance sheet

The reported growth rates are manipulated. In order to do so, the EU's statistical office, EUROSTAT, was forced by the Barroso—Commission 3 years ago to introduce hedonic pricing, meaning that growth can be calculated in a very creative manner: a washing machine which ten years ago had let's say 10 programs today has 20. Under hedonic methods this allows for an adjustment of the figures for quality improvement. Unfortunately, it doesn't mean that more washing machines have been produced and sold. It is easy for a statistical office to show impressive growth rates this way although in reality they are stagnating or even declining. Currently, the industrial production[3] is up by 1.2% in Euro-zone and

---

2.   Eurostat figures for January-July 2007, publication 141/2007 18th October 2007
3.   Eurostat publication 137/2007 12th October 2007

0.9% in EU27 excluding construction. But to know this is worth nothing unless the adjustments being made are laid open. Using the hedonic methods of pricing allow any manipulation Almunia may dream of. In construction, indeed, this is not possible and that's the reason why it is separated from the overall outlook. In the Euro-zone, construction increased by mere 0.4% in August compared with July[4], in the EU27 it was a stunning 1% with the largest increase in the new members Romania (+37%), Slovenia (+31.4%) and Poland (+14.8%) and the largest decreases in Sweden and Germany (-3%). The banks (usually all Western European) in the new member states like they have done it for some 13 years in Ireland financed and over-financed the building bubble so that massive inflation resulting from a self-feeding bubble is now threatening the standard of living of the majority of citizens in those countries. It won't help to tell the people that because of hedonic pricing the economic output were increasing. It is simply not true and the people feel it. The Euro-zone's GDP[5] was up by 0.3% (EU27 +0.5%) in the second quarter of 2007 and some 2.5% (EU 27: +2.8%) compared with the second quarter of 2006 but this is largely owed to the construction sector creating supply overtaking demand by bulk as well as the retail trade, but no real industrial growth. If one ran a company the way the EU Commission is producing manipulated figures one would rather sooner than later end up in front of the bankruptcy judge or in prison.

Copying the US' model of manipulating growth & inflation statistics

The statistical methods employed hide these facts very well.

The US did this for much longer already and much more excessively. In a way, not much growth has been happening in the US in the nineties. All Clinton & Gore created were dotcom bubbles which in the Bush years were wobbling into the real estate market which just recently collapsed. With the help of Al Gore's noble peace prize whatever has been left over from these bubbles will sweep into the green technology industries. All price indexes one finds in the US' Bureau of Economic Analysis in the NIPA (National Income and Product Account) tables about economic growth suggest that without the various adjustments like such for "quality improvements" there was not much of a real growth at all. Nevertheless, the prices were rising while the standard of living is con-

---

4.   Eurostat publication 140/2007 18th October 2007
5.   Eurostat publication 136/2007 11th October 2007

stantly declining. This is what the EU citizens feel as well and they don't want to know why that is but they know that they are being lied to when EU Commissioner Joaquin Almunia is talking about "economic good times". All the growth Almunia celebrates as a big success in Eastern Europe is based on volume in retail trade, meaning that the mostly West German (very few French and British) shopping malls in the new member states are full of the West's top shelf products while the own industrial and agricultural production is sharply declining.

More tricks by the Barroso—Commission: Inflation "officially" at 2.6%

But, the Barroso-Commission also ordered another change in the statistical methods being applied. In order not to show the ever greater disparity between classes of European society in the income statistics as well as in the household savings rate no longer the *medium* but the *median* figures are calculated. The medium figures would include the richest and the poorest quintiles whereas the median figures are reflecting only the middle class households. The growing gulf between rich and poor is not shown in these statistics. It nevertheless does exist and the reality is that the standard of living is declining for most citizens while everything becomes more expensive although the figures show a solid growth and a relatively low inflation. The latter of course only because the consumption basket that used to consist of some 200 goods now counts closer to 600 now containing electronic goods and household items which have relatively become cheaper and by this make up for the increase of products such as butter (+39% since 2001)[6] or fresh vegetables such as broccoli (+64.7%). One may not wish to buy a dish washer every day, but broccoli and other vegetables.

Eurostat's office confirmed to us by an email that hedonic pricing was applied at IT and Audio-Visual equipment. According to Eurostat the prices of such goods has decreased by 13.3%, respectively 10.7% between September 2006 and September 2007[7], but apparently, this does not mean that there is much deflation but that because goods produced this year are considered more advanced than last year's model. It doesn't mean that more of these goods are sold.

---

6.   Financial Times 26th September 2007
7.   Eurostat publication 138/2007 of 16th October 2007

Declining wages, increased prices in restaurants and green grocers

Nevertheless, these figures do have an impact on the calculation of inflation of the consumption basket. These adjustments are at best "creative accounting" but one could also say that by this manipulation the statistics provided are worth nothing. What indeed does show significant increases in inflation are education (+9.1%), tobacco (+5.2%), restaurants and cafés (+3.5%) having the largest weight with 67.8% in the average spending and by this the biggest impact for citizens, whereas the inflation rate in fuels for transport (+4.4%) and cars (+1.2%) have only an impact of 43.7% of weight in the consumption of Europeans. Bread and Cereals (+3.8%) are weighing with 25.4% also a lot, although less than garments (entertainment, theatres, concerts) which only increased by 0.9% but weigh with some 51% have a relevant share in the spending behaviour of citizens across Europe. The increases in the food sector are more significant but people rather cut down on fresh fruits and vegetables which are more than 40% more expensive this year than last year. Healthy nutrition can't be replaced by going to the cinema and also not by buying a car or laptop computer.

It would probably be acceptable if the wages were somewhat in line with the price rises but they are on a sharp decline in major economies such as Germany, Italy and France with for the first time ever after WWII the nominal *and* the net wages showing negative figures in 2004. The declining purchasing power of the Euro has also not done any good despite the strong performance of the Euro against the US Dollar. It would only matter for the citizens if they collectively travelled to the US to enjoy going on a shopping spree.

II.

The East Side Story

The East Side Story
Good news—Bad news

◆

EU government deficit fell to 1.5%, GDP deficit to 1.6% Social Cuts, Privatisations and lowering standard in public services

October—November 2007

First the good news: the Government deficit in the Euro-zone has fallen in 2006 from 2.5% to 1.5% and in the EU 27 from 2.4% to 1.6%. Unfortunately, the government debt increased in absolute terms. This sounds contradicting. But the debts will always increase unless there is a surplus, like it had been in Ireland during the "Celtic Tiger" property boom. Even if a state's (primary)[1] budget is balanced there will be new debts as the interest for the remaining debt has to be paid as well. Luckily, GDP market prices were sine 2003 constantly increasing in both, the Euro-zone (a bit stronger) and (rather modestly) in the EU 27[2]. In other words: good dealing and wheeling in the Euro-zone which can account for a huge export, especially from Germany, to the Eastern European member states. The main reason, why the EU 27 also has some growth to report is because the UK was doing quite well economically—until someone blew up Northern Rock to become Northern Pebbles instead. The real effects of the August 11th—financial turmoil will be felt a bit later. The government debt ratio to the GDP in the EU 27 is declining but one has to consider that the Eastern European countries had minimal debt when they joined but built this up quickly because of the trade deficits. Before the former socialist countries joined the EU, most of them had

---

1. the budget of a state includes interest payments and if such was balanced no additional debt would be accumulated
2. Eurostat publication 142/2007 22nd October 2007

enjoyed a positive trade balance, now it is negative as goods are imported from the West (mainly Germany) while the own agricultural and industrial production has been downsized. Especially the agricultural sector can not compete with the highly subsidized Western European productions. Poland in particular was disappointed when it had to learn that it would never be eligible for the same subsidies the French, Irish, Spanish and even British farmers were granted. Here a double standard was applied which may explain why Poland, traditionally a farming country, woke up with a sore head after the accession celebrations of May 2004 and only a year later voted a Euro-sceptic government into power.

The wave of de-industrialisation in the Eastern European member states followed a wave of job-imports. Because of the lower wages, Western European manufacturers opened production plants in the East.

Expansion nothing but a change of ownership

In contrast to the kind of 'hostile take-over' of the GDR by West Germany in 1990 we can say that this process was already well under way for several years when East European state holdings were privatised and in most cases sold to Western European "investors". In the financial sector of Poland and Czech Republic one can say that more than 70% of the banks are now owned by the West European banks, in Hungary 60% and in Slovakia 80%. German wholesaler Metro and car manufacturers like VW and Audi are aggressively gaining significant market shares.

But the EU expansion not only means that West European companies and shareholders are benefiting from profit maximisation but also receive the bulk of the EU subsidies paid to the new member states. This leads to the perverse situation that the taxpayers in West European countries finance the transfer of jobs to the East while in the new member states the medium sized manufacturers and retailers are ruined. Agricultural as well as industrial production is on a sharp decline in all new member states while the double digit growth rates let EU Economic Affairs Commissioner Joaquin Almunia become indulgent. But, the "growth" is only happening in the retail sector, meaning that citizens in the East are all consuming top shelf products produced in the West while their own industries are at best degraded to providing cheap labour. Labour costs are in many countries only a fraction of those in Germany or any other West European countries. An hour's work in Lithuania for instance costs only 2.42 €, in Estonia 3.03 €, in Poland 4.48 €, in Slovenia 8.98 € including social costs, a bargain compared to Western European costs of roughly 20 € per hour. Not only has this lead to a job transfer towards to the East and by this let unemployment in the "old" EU hit the ceiling but also to the collapse of medium sized companies in the East which can not compete with the wholesalers and major production companies from the West. The total manufacturing working on orders figures show huge surpluses in Czech Republic, Estonia, Latvia, Poland, Hungary and Romania. Jobs are lost in France, Germany (but is doing slightly better again), Denmark, Sweden, Italy, the Netherlands (recovering modestly), and Belgium. For the UK there was no data available. The industrial new orders were up by 5.1% in the Euro-zone and by 8.2% in the EU 27 in August 2007 compared with the same month of the previous year.

This clearly shows that the East is finally overtaking the West, but unfortunately not so much by own industries and productive SME's but rather in becoming the cheap labour production plant. Nevertheless, major Western European retailers not only open their supermarket chains in the East but also provide the products, a situation we have already observed when the GDR was (in 1990) taken over by West Germany.

Germany's industries have now achieved by economic means what Hitler had failed to achieve by military terrorism and torture: the ultimate rule over Europe. The wall which once marked a painful separation of our people no longer exists between East and West, it is now between top and bottom of Europe's societies and even less penetrable for the vast majority of the 457 million citizens.

The price to be paid for being debt-free

So, the absolute numbers of government debt show an increase, while the government expenditure percentage wise continuously decreases. This is also because the GDP in Western Europe grows but although the strict austerity criteria of the Maastricht accord had let social democratic, socialist and labour governments in the late nineties and early 2000s go with the chainsaw through the social net, the government revenue has remained relatively steady. The rising indirect taxes (VAT and 'ecological' taxes) could not completely make up for the tax advantages granted to major corporations as well as the tax relief for the Ultra-High-Net-Worth-Individuals. While the income and corporate tax quota is sharply declining because of these lucrative tax breaks, the indirect taxes are on the rise. At the same time government expenditure is constantly declining showing that the Lisbon strategy is working although it requests brutal cuts in social spending and public services, leading to privatisations or closing down of hospitals, schools, universities, public transport, libraries and theatres.

West Balkan states on the line

October 2007

The atmosphere was friendly as usual when EU Commission President José Manuel Barroso meets a loyal head of government which doesn't give him too much of a headache. And, with the Slovenian government being "fully committed" (Barroso) to the EU enlargement process he can even be more relieved as most of the business on the ground will now be left to the Slovenian Prime Minister Jansez Jansa who pledged to "help" the former Yugoslavian republics to become EU members if they adhered to the same principles as his government did. This sounds nice but what are these principles? First of all it is the Maastricht accord which requires a member state which wishes to adopt the single currency, the Euro, to execute a strict regime of fiscal austerity. Usually, this is only manageable if one cuts down on social standards and public services, privatises public subsistence and "liberalises" the own market. In the case of Slovenia it has worked that well, that since joining the EU the flourishing trade balance has turned negative as Slovenia is, like all other Eastern European member states importing top shelf products from the Euro-zone, mostly from (West) German industries while their own industrial production is reduced to manufacturing intermediate products for the Western European corporations who enjoy cheaper production costs due to low wages and social costs in the East. The growth rate of 5.7% which EU Commission president Barroso congratulated the Prime Minister of Slovenia on is to be seen under the light of predominantly volume of retail trade growing (which means that more is consumed, but exclusively western European goods) as well as construction which like a red-line leads through all growth-regions in poorer parts of the EU. By financing construction and building booms inflation rises as the prices for apartments and houses rise dramatically across the EU. The bubble of the "construction bubble junkies" as the Financial Times calls the beneficiaries of the unhealthy development will eventually collapse. Prime Minister Jansa who will be president of the European Council from January 2008 on is eager to bring the enlargement process in the West Balkans to a positive conclusion as he vowed today. For this, his government has opened a centre for supporting the aspiring new members in Ljubljana and advising them on how to comply with EU principles. The question, however, is whether Slovenia can really pose as a good example in economic terms as not only the trade deficit is mounting higher and higher since joining the EU in 2004, but as it is the first country of the new member states which adopted the Euro in January of this year, has since then managed to bring down it's share of total GDP of the EU down to 0% as the Financial Times noted on 26ᵗʰ September 2007. Even during the dark times of being a communist Yugoslavia, Slovenia had a better stand with neighbouring Western European countries in this regard.

This may explain why Serbia which is more than reluctant to let itself be overrun by Western Europe is not willing to sign more than a soft association agreement, SAA, tomorrow with EU enlargement Commissioner Olli Rehn.

At the brink of Fascism

What happens when citizens are not feeling taken care of by their political leadership can be observed in Eastern Europe lately: disenfranchised citizens are more and more often turning towards the right. In many countries populist fascist groups are on the rise as DER SPIEGEL reported[1]. The radical *Jobbik Party* in Hungary founded the *Magyar Garda,* a radical SA—like group to which the leader of the parliamentary opposition in Budapest, Viktor Orban, does not keep much of a distance.

In Slovakia it is the Slovak National Party of Jan Slota which may make one feel a cold shower run down the back. But in some countries there are the extreme left also becoming stronger like in Czech Republic which caused the infuriated Topolanek—government to ban the Communist youth organisation.

Once they got rid off Stalinism most Eastern Europeans may have thought of their nations as their mothers and the EU as their lover. Now, they had to learn that the lover never is a good replacement for the mother.

---

1.   21ˢᵗ October 2007 SPIEGEL online

III.

Narkozy and others

Sarkozy faces truth

✦

The Hour of the populists?

In Speech in front of the European Parliament criticises financial markets

October 2007

President Nicolas Sarkozy of France is not known for being a declared anti-capitalist. Nevertheless, he offered to the Members of the European Parliament a flamboyant criticism of the "speculators who are responsible for the financial turmoil" that Monsieur Sarkozy emphasised were "not supported by the citizens of the world in seeking further excesses".

Recently, the French president has clashed with both, the EU Commission as well as the European Central Bank who rejected any interference by the French government in the policy of the ECB by reminding him of the independence of the Frankfurt based institution which is to a large degree modelled on the German Bundesbank. In addition, EU Economics and Monetary Affairs Commissioner Joaquin Almunia in an unusual harsh tone told Mr. Sarkozy "to take a leaf from the book of the Germans" in regards to learning how to restructure the economy and make France a success story returning to the growth rates of the nineties and early 2000s. In those years France had better growth rates than Germany and also a trade surplus. Nowadays, the French GDP[1] only grows by 1.3% while Germany is up at 2.5%, followed by the Netherlands (+2.4%), Italy (1.8%). Outside the Euro-zone growth rates look even more enticing, i.e. in the UK with 3% GDP growth and the Eastern European Member States with even bigger growth rates, although these are predominantly owed to a steady increase of volume in retail trade which results from imports of West European (mostly German) products. Here, France looses out as the trade deficit now accounts for some 25 billion Euros during the first three quarters of 2007[2] while Germany is

---

1.   Eurostat publication 136/2007

celebrating a record trade surplus of 114.9 billion Euros in the same time. France got a structural problem as 90% of it's export is accounted for by the CAC 40 listed major corporations. French SMEs are marginalised. Mr. Sarkozy's fierce stand-off against the "international speculators and financial sharks" seems to be intended to divert attention from his governments failure to boost growth in France by increasing the industrial production which in August was down to 0.3% compared to 1.7% in July 2007[3] while Germany after weak performances in the previous years all of a sudden sees a growth of 1.7% in August shunning previously stagnating Italy with 1.3%. The figures for total manufacturing on orders look even more dramatic with a recorded decline by 2.7% for French SME's while the German medium sized entrepreneurs can benefit from the economic up-swing resulting from expansion into Eastern Europe and enjoy a growth of 1.4%, while Italy slows down by—0.6%[4]. Again, Eastern European members are accounting for bigger growth rates than France: Latvia (+8.2%), Poland (+4.9%), Czech Republic (+4.3%), Estonia (+4.0%) and Romania (+2.3%) while it has to be noted that the cheap labour and lower social costs in those countries attracts a lot of Western European (mostly German) companies who let the Eastern European workers produce intermediate products while the own production in those countries has been downsized by a wave of de-industrialisation following the radical liberalisations demanded by the EU Commission before admitting accession. One may call it also "Post-Accession—Syndrome" as a closer scrutiny of the contribution of the EU 27 to Extra EU 27—trade[5] reveals. Germany and Austria are the only beneficiaries with 7.4 billion Euros, and 0.7 billion Euros respectively, growth while all others are either stagnating or showing negative figures: Estonia (0), Czech Republic (-0.3), Latvia (-0.1), Hungary (-0.6) and Poland (-0.8), while France only gains 0.6 billion Euros with the UK trailing by record—5.8 billion Euros due to uncompetitive exchange rates raising the question whether they would do better to either join the Euro or even leave the European Union and rather join NAFTA. And even in the most profitable field of construction business the output of Germany is 2.0% (mostly STRABAG building infrastructure in Eastern member states) and the Dutch ING both earning most of the EU subsidies allowing the Netherlands to have some 2.5% growth France shows a weak performance of only 0.4%. In other words: France is loosing out in all important areas of business and suffers from

---

2.   Eurostat publication 141/2007
3.   Eurostat publication 137/2007
4.   Eurostat publication 143/2007.
5.   Eurostat publication 141/2007

having missed out on the benefits of conquering the markets in the East. To blame the financial markets which in reality have nothing to do with the French malaise is the populist's approach. The same could be said about cutting down on social standards in France which not only provoke paralysing strike and industrial actions but might lead to a pro-cyclical development Mr. Sarkozy should not wish to create in a situation like this as domestic demand could collapse. At present, France still shows positive household savings rates[6] indicating a balanced social account which also let's France have a higher birth rate than Germany and most other EU members except for Ireland. If, as a result from social cuts proposed by Mr. Sarkozy the French are de-saving to finance consumption, they might as well enter a cul-de-sac. Germany only sees some positive figures in it's household savings rates because of the overhaul of the pension system by the Schröder-government which reduced state transfers while providing for tax breaks for private pension plans. In reality, this does not mean that German citizens are really saving more than before, but they just try to compensate by private contribution what the state now denies them now. As a result, people in Germany are saving less than in 2000, which actually means that the *real* savings rate is constantly shrinking in real terms as inflation eats into it. Also EU-wide, the savings rate in 2006 is at the level of 2000, while this in real terms means that because of inflation, people have not saved but de-saved. Because of shrinking savings Germans also spend less. Domestic demand declined and only recently showed a modest recovery. France should be careful when weighing it's options as Germany in this regard doesn't pose for a positive example. For the French president to blame the unfortunate economic development of France on either the "evil financial speculators" or the ECB and EU Commission is as far fetched as populists usually argue.

---

6.   Eurostat publication 073/2007

Inflation hits ceiling

◆

"Consumption" basket now contains electronic goods. Real Inflation for food at 25%. Why strong Euro hurts France more than Germany.

October 2007

There aren't any good news from neither the financial markets nor the EU Commission although the latter maintains that generally EU citizens were "enjoying economic good times" as EU Economic and Currency Affairs Commissioner Joaquin Almunia reiterates at every occasion. He is still trying to sell the Euro as a success story. Meanwhile, Eurostat, the EU's statistical office estimates the Eurozone's Inflation to rise further. It was 2.6% in October, up from 2.1% in September. Alex Weber, the Bundesbank President and an important voice at the European Central Bank (ECB) as well as Jürgen Starke, the ECB's chief economist, lament that the inflation might go up to 3% by the end of the year. Well, it was not so much the central bank itself which hugely contributed to this by lowering the interest rates in the previous years again and again. It has rather been the income distribution which has led to the bubble building. Neoclassical ideologists always want to draw the attention on the central banks to be responsible but it is rather that investment banks have created an incredible amount of very creative financial products such as derivatives which inflated and only made the owners of big money rich and richer. By this irresponsible behaviour the investment bankers let the amount of money, M 3, grow to become a for any central banker uncontrollable bubble. In March 2007 it had already been with a plus of 8 billion Euros some 10.9% well above the previous year's craziness. Said bubble was needed by the investment banks to issue their dubious financial instruments which now pose a big problem, but also the private equity firms went on a bonanza in the style of "buy it-strip it-scrap it-sell it". The wobbling financial bubble financed all these take over transactions in the late nineties and early 2000s.

Trichet's Dilemma: he can't serve citizens *and* shareholders likewise

Now, Jean Claude Trichet, the President of the European Central Bank has to deal with the mistakes of the past. He is in quite a dilemma right now as inflation is usually brought under control by the central bank raising interest rates. As the United States' Federal Reserve just lowered it's base rate last week in order to bail out the ailing financial institutions suffering from their self-made malaise of the real-estate bubble, the Euro has reached an all time high against the US Dollar. If Trichet now raises the real interest it means that the Euro becomes even stronger, and by this hurts the Euro-zone's export. Somehow, France is threatened by this more than the export champion of the EU, Germany. The explanation is quite simple: The German industry receives many intermediate products from outside the Euro-zone, i.e. from Eastern European member states which produce under the auspices of the German industries. In this way Germany even benefits from the strong Euro as it makes it's productions in the subsidiaries of the German industries in Eastern Europe even cheaper. France does not have that many subsidiary productions outside the Euro-zone. And, the other reason for the German export industry not suffering as much from the strong performance of the Euro as any other member state is that Germany mostly exports capital goods, such as electronics from let's say Siemens or cars from BMW, VW, Porsche, Mercedes but also war technology the buyers of which will not turn to other goods that swiftly. France instead exports predominantly consumption goods such as wine, cheese, fashion, and agricultural products and by this feels much more the strong wind against it. This is the reason why French President Nicolas Sarkozy is against further interest rate increases while Germany's shareholders rather see it cool and want the ECB to get inflation under control since it poses the only threat to their valuables.

Manipulated Statistics: "Consumption" Basket contains cars and washing machines

And, how is the ordinary citizen affected? Well, inflation up to 3% is within the margin of the Maastricht stability criteria. Theoretically, it should be no big problem, but somehow the current inflation is felt much more by consumers. Because the "food" basket now also contains washing machines, cars, electronic goods, digital cameras, laptop computers as well as clothes which all have become cheaper and not only bred, butter, milk, vegetables and fruits, the nominal inflation can be kept at a lower than actual level. The problem is: One does not buy a washing machine or PC every day but may want to have fresh vegetables and fruits which last but not least become increasingly a luxury good because of the bio-fuel production. The real inflation in the food sector is rather at 25–30% in the Euro-zone with butter being at a record high of 39% more than in 2006 in Germany. But also energy costs rose dramatically, not only because of the high oil prices, but also because the recent privatisations and take-overs have created private monopolies which according to a German government study published last week were engaged in price-fixing. In 2006 energy prices for gas, electricity and heating fuel rose by 9.5%. Electricity costs today 46% more than in 2000. This is only partly owed to the high oil prices otherwise the balance sheets of E.on, RWE and other now private energy consortia would not show double digit profits. "Ecological" taxes rose by 41% after the "liberalisation" which began in Germany with the red-green government of Chancellor Gerhard Schröder in 1998. If one doesn't want to sit in a cold and dark apartment the consumer has no choice but to pay. The citizen will cut down elsewhere, maybe on buying broccoli.

High inflation in the food sector poses a major problem for everyone who is predominantly buying his basis subsistence goods rather than electronic goods, washing machines or cars. It means that the standard of living is declining. The day will come that even Mr. Almunia will understand that one can not eat a digital camera and that inflation is a threat to society as it is a fight over ownership.

Sarkozy's 360° turn

✦

French Master of Pirouettes

From Neo Classical to Neo-Interventionist?
Clashes with ECB over French Traditionalism

September 2007

French President Nicolas Sarkozy has so far rather been known for his neo-classical approach than for being a traditional Gaullist. In a way, the Germans force Sarkozy to become a state interventionist against his own conviction. He is now left with the task to rescue France from Germany. De Gaulle would turn in his grave if he saw what and how Sarkozy was doing it.

It is certainly not easy for Mr. Sarkozy to maintain his neo-classical approach while at the same time trying to remain his popularity. His first few months as president have won him an equal share of applause as well as criticism. Much has been written about his surprise-style of setting the agenda often leaving followers and opponents with their mouth wide open. What has been clear from the very beginning was that this president is not a socialist, a strong advocate of liberalisation and self determination. President Sarkozy managed to divide the working class and employees of his country by attempting to break up the solidarity model. Many young, employed, French citizens saw that their social contributions were weighing heavy on their wages and by offering to reduce such significantly he won their hearts. He will be popular with them as long as they are not going to be unemployed, fall sick or become old. The new 'flexibility' of the workforce just follows Germany in it's labour market reform pushed through by the government of Social-Democratic chancellor Gerhard Schröder. The radical reform is now bearing fruits: 1 million new jobs were created, unfortunately the bulk of these outside the usual tariff scheme negotiated between employers and unions and by this providing a certain standard of social security.

Holy cows to be slaughtered by those who once fed them

The post war West—German success model was based on a socially balanced free market economy but today less than 60% of German employment contracts are governed by the tariff scheme and the number of jobs created by recruitment agencies is on a sharp increase. The misperception is that these agencies create new jobs. They don't. They only manage to replace existing well paid and protected jobs with 'flexible arrangements'. The jobs which are newly created are low paid, bearing only minimal social benefits. The owners of such recruitment agencies of course make a lot of money with leasing out 'their' workforce. One may debate the legitimacy of such a system and the benefit to society. What should have caused an outcry is the fact that Wolfgang Clement, former labour minister in the Schröder-government is now on the board of Germany's largest recruitment agency. In a way, the legislation brought in by Schröder and Clement directly benefited those companies. Like conservative chancellor Helmut Kohl was not willing to touch the principles such as a certain social balance of the West-German cushioned capitalism, Gaullist President Jacques Chirac didn't dare to commit himself to a crackdown. In Germany, this has only become possible with a Social-Democratic government. The holy cows had to be slaughtered by those who once fed them. In France the establishment didn't trust the conditioner-washed socialists but brought a populist to power.

A government brought down to it's knees

Now, Sarkozy who saw the de Villepin—cabinet be brought down to it's knees by student protests has to do it. Only a strong and powerful president like Nicolas Sarkozy can push through the neo-liberal agenda and so far he managed quite well not to be seen as serving other than the French people's genuine interests. In the aftermath of the financial crisis of 11th August he openly criticised the ECB for 'collaborating with speculators' although all Jean-Claude Trichet was doing was to avert a financial meltdown by offering liquidity on tender basis. The money was pumped into the market, but it never reached the man in the street, so there was no danger of inflation or of an increased M3 as those funds had to be paid back within days and were even bearing interest. One can hardly speak of the ECB bailing out banks which speculated and lost. The 'Northern Rock' case in the UK indeed can be seen as a rescue mission Prime Minister Gordon Brown who was flirting with the opinion polls amid speculation that he might call elections. But, President Sarkozy launches his attacks against the ECB to divert attention from domestic problems. He knows that the EURO is not very popular with the French citizens. A poll published by the Financial times in January of this year indicated that the vast majority of French citizens would rather see the Franc come back and led to at that time presidential candidate Nicolas Sarkozy openly question the independence of the European Central Bank. "Bitter Union. Gallic gripes create strains in Euro-zone" the Financial Times headlined and quoted French politicians saying that there should be room for "pulling various macro-economic levers—fiscal policy, the exchange rate and interest rates—in a co-ordinated way". This prompted in chancellor Angela Merkel harshly rejecting any change in the status of the ECB and said she was "greatly concerned". Now, President Sarkozy does not leave any opportunity pass to criticise the ECB for their policy to help the markets as he sees that speculators are bailed out by Trichet. This may appear a bit hypocritical as he himself has become president on the back of Vincent Bolloré, the media tycoon and construction giant who very actively had participated in the bubble building of the financial markets.

Sarkozy's shadow—boxing

Nicolas Sarkozy is clever enough to win opinion polls by pleasing the people by popular statements while at the same time doing the opposite. His shadow boxing over the role of the ECB prompted the EU Commission to react in an equally unusual harsh tone. EU Currency and Economic Affairs Commissioner Joaquin Almunia suggested France could take a leaf out of the books of Austria and Germany, which have significantly improved their global competitiveness. The commissioner does not mention of course, that Germany is suffering from a collapse in domestic demand (-7.6% in volume of retail trade in the first half of 2007) due to constantly declining wages resulting from Schröder's Agenda 2010 labour market liberalisation to which two thirds of Germans are today opposed to. Since the launch of the Euro in 1999 France has performed better than Germany which had tumbling growth rates while France enjoyed between 2 and 3% of annual growth. But those good days are gone and Mr. Sarkozy is aware of it. He needs to bring the French economy back on track but his attacks against the ECB are unjustified and can only be seen as populist.

The hour of the populist:
a double Rittberger—pirouette

That's why most of the Eurozone's 13 governments as well as the European Commission and ECB were "unhappy about Mr Sarkozy's public criticism of the ECB's handling of global market turbulence and his equally public demands for interest rate cuts" the Financial Times noted. On the other hand, even an energy bundle of a president like Nicolas Sarkozy is not able to govern as he wants. He has to take care of France and protect it's assets. That's why he waved through the energy mergers of Electricité de France (EDF) and Gaz de France (GDF) as otherwise the cookie monster in form of German energy conglomerates would eat them.

"French Energy mergers test Europe's free market puritans" the Financial Times headlined and continued saying that "Nicolas Sarkozy is viewed as his country's most liberal politician but his policies hearken back to an era of state intervention". Well, this cast suspicion over his industrial activism, to say the least. On the other hand, France has a problem with it's Small and Medium Enterprises (SMEs). According to the Frankfurter Allgemeinen Zeitung (FAZ)[1] the great export performance of a few major corporations is obstructing a clear view on France's medium sized industries which is staying well behind such CAC 40 companies like Airbus or Pharma industries Sanofi Aventis. Nowadays, 10% of the 100,000 French exporting companies account for 95% of the export. Overall, while exports are still growing but at reduced rates, the imports are rising much steeper leading to a record foreign trade deficit of 26.5 billion Euros in 2006 but in the first six months of 2007 a new record number of 15.3 billion Euros has been reached. Germany instead has achieved a trade surplus of 97 billion Euros in the same time, proving that all the German Aufschwung (up-swing) is about is export, so Nicolas Sarkozy would be well advised to rather concentrate on improving the situation for the SMEs than only listening to his buddies from the CAC 40 listed major corporations. And, if he wants to avoid the mistakes Germany has made with it's labour market reforms which led to a harsh decline in domestic demand, he better does not apply too many of the old fashioned neoclassical tools. Populism is always short-lived and the ECB can't help him in doing his homework, nor is the central bank in Frankfurt responsible for the malaise of the French medium sized industries the government seems to have forgotten about.

---

1.   FAZ 10th September 2007 „Frankreich: Sorgenkind Industrie"

Take the money and run!

◆

Legal Money Laundering doubles.

April 2007

The good news (as usual) first: the direct investment into the EU 27 from outside has risen in the last year by 20%. Every finance minister would be happy about this influx of foreign capital. It strengthens the economy, boosts growth, creates jobs and increases currency reserves and overall stability. That's at least the theory. Now, the reality: The figures EUROSTAT published two weeks ago and put a smile on the face of EU Economic and Currency Affairs Commissioner Joaquin Almunia reveal that also the EU's foreign direct investment had enjoyed an enormous increase by stunning 38% in 2006. One may still be cheerful about that figure if one believes what the EU Commission as well as European Central bank try to hammer into our heads: that it was good that the EU invested elsewhere and for instance took over foreign companies like Daimler did it with Chrysler or invested in overseas markets. Again, in theory, this would be enticing, even though Daimler in a more desperate than deliberate appearing move amputated Chrysler from itself just recently as the investment had not paid off. However, a closer scrutiny further reveals that the foreign investment of the EU 27 in so called offshore financial centres doubled. In 2005 it was 23 billion Euros, in 2006 just over 47 billion Euros. Now, while one should be careful with prejudices one can conclude that the bulk of the funds are transferred in order to avoid taxes. This is especially true for major industries and their shareholders who move their profits to offshore places not because the weather is nicer. The financial institutions in such places only exist because they assist in more or less legal money laundering. The EUROSTAT figures also show that the main growth coming in investments from offshore financial centres also doubled in the last 12 months: were it in 2005 18 billion Euros it were in 2006 37 billion. In other words: our major corporations legally avoid tax by transferring billions of the profit out of the EU to an offshore bank which they probably collectively own only to grant themselves a loan which they can declare as a foreign investment made into their company for which they can deduct the interest and once profits are increased pay out royalties to their "foreign investors" which they are themselves. If an ordinary citizen wants to do the same the squad cars, revenue commissioner and criminal assets bureau detectives would raid his home and launch a money laundering investigation. But, the tax laws have evidently not been written by the have-nots but by those who can spin the big wheel. At the same time, indirect consumer taxes are steadily increasing while the Small & Medium Sized Entrepreneur (SME) are not left with any choice but to pay their dues as only multinational corporations are able to use the offshore construction effectively. Thus the state is pulling coin per coin and note per note the earnings of working people and SMEs out of their pockets. The state knows how to compensate for the Capitalism has given us a lot—after it has taken it from us.

Citizens step in

◆

One more time, the European Parliament missed a chance to execute tax justice

October 2007

When EU Commission President José Manuel Barroso ("JMB") and the current president of the Council, the Portuguese Minister-President Sokrates entered the arena of the Strasbourg Plenary of the European Parliament yesterday morning to praise each other for their "great achievements" in making the Lisbon Treaty which is about to replace the "Constitution" it all carried some surrealistic reminiscence of Soviet era style of self assurance. And, like in the good old Stalinist times the leaders only want to believe what suits them. Otherwise it would be inexplicable why the EU Commission lauded the decision of the conservative and liberal majority in the Economic & Monetary Affairs Committee of the European parliament to vote—out the proposals for harmonisation of income—, corporate and capital gains taxes with a certain minimum tax becoming mandatory in all EU member states, which was contained in the Wagenknecht-report. Such Common Consolidated Corporate Tax base would stop the tax dumping competition among member states.

The income from corporate income taxes in all EU member states fell by 10% in the last ten years and the private capital gains are increasingly privileged by the transition into dual taxation systems. In order to make good on these losses the indirect taxes such as for consumption (VAT), and especially those on energy, fashionably marked 'ecological' taxation, sharply increase. This is a consequence of a tax dumping competition in a single market. One should rather think about the fact that the corporate tax spiral leading much sharper downwards in the EU than in any other OECD country. It can hardly be pinned down to "globalisation", a myth always repeated by the advocates of liberalisation. Especially the income from mere financial transactions could become subject to a harmonised minimum tax, but the EU Commission is quick to denounce it as counterproductive in creating growth and against the tax sovereignty of the member states. For some reason, the EU Commission has no problem with the indirect taxes to be harmonised, i.e. at the highest possible level as one can see when it comes to VAT.

The effective tax quota for the EU DJ STOXX 50 fell from 36.5% in 1988 to 31.4% in 2000, and ranges now at 23.8%. In the OECD it is still at 28%, down from 37% as an average.

On the other hand the share of the payee tax on wages accounts today for 64% of the member state's income whereas 15 years ago this was in the western EU member states around 37%. In the same period, the corporate taxes' share on the total taxes effectively paid declined from 41% to 22%, so in other words, the citizens are more and more stepping in for the tax dodgers who manage to legally (and illegally) evade taxes. By the way, the social contribution across the EU15 as of GDP remained absolutely steady at 11.5% so there was no such thing like an exploding social cost which justified the indirect tax rises, another myth often spread by politicians it is rather that the state needs to get the money from somewhere and if it is no longer possible from corporate and capital gains taxes, it will increasingly be from indirect taxes.

The neo-classical credo that lower taxes lead to investment and the investment to production and ultimately to the creation of jobs is led ad absurdum when one analyses where newly accumulated wealth is derived from: 4/5 stem from capital gains, interest, financial transactions, stocks and shares. In order not to become subject to taxation the owners of such funds "invest" those in off shore places. Of course, other than a few palm trees and banks there are no industries where one could really invest or otherwise make use of the money in those tax havens so the money needs to be re-introduced in the economy of the EU. This is done by so called "financial direct investment" (FDI) which again does not mean that someone really *invests* such funds in any production line but rather wishes to legally enjoy the fruits of the accumulation. In other words: the Financial Direct Investment from offshore places is a legal way to evade taxes. One can also speak of money laundering. In the last year the amount of Financial Direct Investment from offshore places into the EU has doubled as Eurostat reported.

The Eurostat figures also show that the main growth coming in investments from offshore financial centres also doubled in the last 12 months: were it in 2005 18 billion Euros it were in 2006 37 billion. In other words: our major corporations legally avoid tax by transferring billions of the profit out of the EU to an offshore bank which they probably collectively own only to grant themselves a loan which they can declare as a foreign investment made into their company for which they can deduct the interest and once profits are increased pay out royalties to their "foreign investors" which they are themselves. The Small & Medium Sized Entrepreneur (SME) are not left with any choice but to pay their dues as only multinational corporations are able to use the offshore construction effectively.

Another crucial aspect is taxation. Only the indirect taxes, such as VAT, Petrol—, Alcohol, Luxury-Goods Tax etc. shall be harmonised but not the income and corporate taxes. Therefore, the ruining process of tax dumping will be further reinforced. Major corporations will continue to follow the mere logic of investing only in those countries of dwindling tax rates. Member states continue to compete with each other (or break up like Great-Britain which for the simple reason of tax dumping competition have 'independence' movements in Scotland and Wales which for only that reason are supported by industries in the UK) in lowering corporate taxes and in the end no taxes will be paid by those who can effectively evade it.

The treaty of Lisbon makes sure that even if there had been a majority for the proposals for minimum corporate- and capital gains taxes initially contained in the Wagenknecht report it would be overruled by the treaty. The European Parliament at best would see any attempt or executing tax justice being squashed in the European Court of Justice. This shows how much sovereignty the European Parliament really enjoys in these vital issues and it lays bare whose interests were listened to when writing the treaty. That's why JMB and Sokrates were smiling all along when celebrating their 'achievements' together with the conservative and liberal majority in the European Parliament.

Null Ouvert?—Va Banque!

✦

As MiFID comes, the Virtual Reality Casino is open
ECB's Trichet from now on will only move deck chairs on Titanic

New EU Directive less strict than in US in terms of transparency. EU allows investment banks to play roulette with self made tokens. What has proven not to work in the US now becomes standard in an EU gold-plating financial market

The slide show presented by the Director General for Internal Market & Services, Wright, featured an image of a man-eating plant as the opening illustration. Well, whoever chose this image for the slide show introducing the "Markets in Financial Instruments Directive" (MiFID) that has been worked on for some 7 years, must have a good sense of humour.

September 2007

MiFID is replacing the Investment Services Directive. It generally is aimed at making the financial market safer for customers but at the same time the liberalisation across Europe also poses risks as the competition among traditional Stock Exchanges and Investment Banks will drastically increase with no real regulatory body overseeing what is happening in the market which so far had to meet the standards of the national stock exchanges and bourses.

The interest of the investment banks of course is to avoid transaction fees by circumventing the stock exchanges. But, so far the stock exchanges also played a vital role in the control of the market by at least recording the amount and size of transactions while also being able to see potentially overheated or even pro-cyclical developments.

64

All this is gone as of today since the investment banks can offer all financial products such as "Collateralised Debt Obligations" (CDOs) which had lead to the financial crisis culminating on 11th August of this year and so called "Derivatives" which are nothing else but betting tokens.

Like when betting on a horse one only needs a fraction of the amount that is at stake and if one is lucky one can make a fortune within a very short time. Hedge funds are specialised in these transactions. The risks are high, though, and there are many examples for major defaults.

Make sure that all that foam is not presented at the cashier's desk

The only threats to the validity of the foam created artificially are inflation and that's why Bundesbank and ECB have currency stability as their major objective in their policy and masses which one day would question the legitimacy of such bubbles which although being accumulated completely isolated from the real economy on the other hand do have some very real effects on same when it comes to their owners wishing to consume what they deem rightfully earned.

Every Dollar or Euro being multiplied on the Roulette tables of the virtual reality casino of the financial markets can be used for buying goods in the real economy in the same way as a Dollar or Euro which has been worked for by producing a good. Therefore, the masses who are working for their money might ask why they should let the money won in the derivative betting scene and "investment" bankers be allowed to be used for anything else but gambling. This, of course, would mean to issue tokens rather than real coins and notes to those "bubble junkies" (as the Financial Times calls them). After all, if their bubbles burst it does have drastic consequences for the real economy as we have seen in the aftermath of 11th August which not only blew up Northern Rock to pieces but also slowed down the economy in the UK and across Europe while also fuelling inflation and will lead to mass unemployment although a slight recovery of the economy had been seen just weeks before.

Operating from the shadows

Hedge funds do not have to show their assets but can virtually create whatever financial instruments they want as long as they find somebody to buy it from them. It's like the good old chain-letter system we all played in school: as long as you find someone who is more gullible than yourself and pays an even higher price for air in a hot tin than you did, the game goes on. In case of the hedge funds it is even worse: they can gamble with derivatives worth 25 times their own assets base (which no one can control). The EU Commission's demand for a self—imposed correctness and business ethics sounds a bit hollow when it comes to the question as to who is exercising the control and polices the MiFID regulations. The truth is: nobody.

Like the Private Equity market, which financed the firework of all these take over transactions, derivatives originated in the US. Hedge funds were only admitted to the continental European market in 2004 but since have overtaken the US markets by volume.

Investment banks, the classification is a bit misleading, they should rather be called Groupiers, do like the over-the counter-transactions because these are not reflected in the balance sheets, on the other hand this poses a threat to the whole financial system since these "products" are not appearing in the relevant statistics and by this are uncontrollable.

For the central bankers, the ECB especially, the fact that the amount of circulating money, M 3, can no longer be brought under control, poses an even bigger problem as all their classical monetary tools loose their power.

Hedge funds do not have to lay bare their assets, and if they have to they collapse, as we witnessed on 11th August.

Wright: "New types of platforms"

Now, as MiFID becomes effective, these "Investment" banks will finally take over all of the financial markets while stock exchanges become increasingly irrelevant. Mr. Wright expects a boom in those over-the-counter—transactions like we have seen it after the London market had been liberalised, he explained. MiFID also provided for "new types of platforms and investment banks in a widened market".

In reality this means that Stock exchanges will be replaced by investment banks concentrating on over-the-counter—transactions. Online gambling and betting seems to be the credo of our times. Where is the good old European banker's tradition gone? Where has the 'normal' business of lending and managing savings in a responsible way gone? The investment banks are certainly not able to look after their clients in any responsible way at all.

Those savers in the US who had 10,000 US Dollars before August 11th in a private pension fund tied to a hedge fund after 11th August now only have 2,000

Dollars. One should not forget that these are the life-time savings people have worked for which are gambled with.

The Hedge Fund Junkies

"Long Term Capital Management" (LTMC), the infamous hedge fund, which had been betting after the South East Asian crisis of summer 1997 on a swift recovery was caught on the wrong foot when a few weeks later Russia declared itself bankrupt. LTMC who had only "invested" some 6 billion US-Dollars in order to spin a wheel of 125 billion sank quicker than the Titanic.

Richard Buck Staber, at that time one of the key players at LTCM, in 1997 had thought that the spreads would after the Asian crisis rebound, but then the Russian financial crisis kicked in.

"Get out of my way!" the investment bankers shout

And, Mr. Wright made it almost furiously clear, that the EU Commission's clientele is not willing to accept any excuses for not implementing MiFID right a way. Like a boy who was taken away his toys he angrily said that "We will prosecute those who do not comply" but seemed to realise that his tone sounded too aggressive so he corrected his harsh words and also softened his voice and said "we will launch infringement proceedings against those states who do not implement MiFID within the next few months". Then, Mr. Wright praised the new directive again for demanding from the investment bankers to "do what is best for the client" and not to sell products they want to get rid off. The problem may as well be, that the broker, banker or consultant advising the client doesn't even know himself what is a good and safe opportunity or not.

The transparency is a joke compared with the US and even Mr. Wright agrees: "MiFID does not contain as strong rules of disclosure like in the US" Mr. Wright admitted. That means that investment banks in the EU can hide how much capital and what an assets base they really have. And, the USA is even stricter regulated than London.

London is main "over-the-counter" market in Europe.

It should be prohibited as it destabilises not only the financial markets but also the real economy as in reaction to the financial meltdown banks are tightening their credit policy so in the end the SMEs may suffer from the restrictive policy of the banks to grant loans. Production comes to a halt.

EU Commission eager to push through the final deregulations

The EU Commission is certainly aware of that and tries to set forth an ambitious target for compliance making the investment bankers and brokers agree to "do the best for the client" as if it would help to emphasise that.

Of course a broker or investment banker who earns a commission on selling financial products has an interest in the transaction, so how can one make sure that his client's interest comes first?

The EU Commission's mantra of competition sorting it out and their plea to the financial services industry to please behave and be good is where the Commission is weakest. It can only plea not to become too excessive but it gives the major players the tools to do what they want. Back in February of this year I asked Internal Market Commissioner Charles McGreevy, an accountant by profession, whether one should not control the major firms in order to make sure that no fraud or excessive abuse could destabilise the system.

"What a mega bureaucracy that should control all this I had on my mind" Charley McGreevy retorted. Well, what happens when one does not control it and leaves it up to the 'industry' to control itself, we have seen on 11th August of this year, when the first of a series of crashes destabilised the financial markets and will still continue as there are some 128 billion USD of such commercial papers still to be presented until January 2008.

And, of course, when they got it wrong, exactly the same banks and shareholders who always hate the state to "interfere" with the "business interests in a free market" by any kind of regulation are not shy to call on the public to bail them out like in the Northern Rock case. We will see some more like this to come in the next few weeks as there are some 3,000 billion Dollars CDO and other commercial papers out there and no one knows at the moment who holds those, when they will be presented at the cashier's desk and what will happen if the banks have to take them onto their balance sheets.

Then, it is over with over-the-counter-transactions, right when continental Europe has overtaken the US and London by volume.

Foreseeable disaster: Threats as severe as in 1929

But, one could have known that this will happen one day. Over the years the central banks have flooded the markets with cheap money and by this made the rich richer. Now, there is a threat of inflation which will first make the poor poorer.

Even European Central Bank President Jean-Claude Trichet at the Davos meetings spoke of "potentially unstable conditions" and that "there is now such creativity of new and very sophisticated financial instruments ... that we don't know fully where the risks are located." Frightening to think that the chief financial officer of the world's largest currency has to admit that he has no clue what is going on: "We are trying to understand what is going on but it is a big, big challenge." Trichet is quoted by the Financial Times on 29th January 2007.

It would be time to ask these officials who they think they are representing. And, especially, in whose interests they are acting.

In a time where the world economy is facing threats as severe as the black Monday in 1929 and at least as deep than the black Friday of 1987, the EU Commission has nothing else to do but to enhance the flickering fire by further deregulation. Just before a collapse is imminent like a flickering oil lamp which burns even brighter just before it extinguishes, a firework of skyrocketing profits can be observed in the financial markets.

Nervous Central Bankers, cool EU officials

Alex Weber, the German Bundesbank President and as such a member in the board of the ECB warned last Sunday that "we are worried about a rise of prices in many sectors, not only energy and food.

By the end of the year, inflation could be at 3%." This, indeed, would constitute the largest increase in Germany for over 14 years. The chief economist of the ECB, Jürgen Stark, in addition warns of inflation in conjunction with an ailing economy which is slowed down by the strong Euro.

The combination of inflation and a slowing economy is the nightmare of any central banker. It means a rise of unemployment, lower state revenue and increasing poverty. The global deregulation—wave has lead to today's capitalism showing a similar beauty as the capitalism of the first half of the twentieth century which had burnt itself in an unprecedented way into the collective memory of everyone who had survived the century's political and cultural upheavals.

There are definitely memories one doesn't want to revive. Mr. Wright's slide show ended and who ever in his office had selected the images has by now probably been handed his papers as the last slide Mr. Wright, the Director General of the EU Commission for Internal Market, showed vessel looking like the Titanic but with the name "MiFID" on it, but, as Mr. Wright noted, just three and not four chimneys. Well, if that's the only difference....

Green light for Hedge Funds

✦

EP passes Van den Burg Report

June 2007

Hedge funds in the past have been widely criticised even by conservative politicians. They have become immensely unpopular in the eyes of the public as the turn over of such money spinners not only exceeds many state's budgets but because such volume can put any government be it a democracy or a dictatorship under pressure. Even in the EU hedge fund managers have more power than any elected political representative. A government will hardly implement a law to regulate the financial markets if a hedge fund threatens to withdraw billions of Dollars or Euros from the country's financial markets. Hedge funds do not produce anything. They are fed by financial products such as derivatives or MTN's (medium term notes) that do not create anything, do not use any tool, no energy (other than a small amount of electricity to run the computer systems of this virtual reality casino) and do not require much labour input. On the other hand, the gains are astronomical and not only exceed growth rates of productive industries but accumulate wealth beyond any realistic economic raise in productivity. As virtual this bubble of virtual reality money is, as dangerous it is for the financial markets which are continuously flooded by these hedge funds. The problem is not that some Ultra High Net Worth Individuals (as Merrill Lynch refers to the few multi-billionaire who own and control half of this planet's economic output) are gambling in their casinos and pile up electronically stored numbers and zeroes, but this artificially created wealth relates to the production in a dreadful way: the money can be spent although it has not been worked for. An unhealthy situation every economist from Adam Smith to Karl Marx to John Maynard Keynes would outright reject. Now, the problem is also not that someone bathes in Champagne every day, raises his kids with a silver spoon in their mouth and buys 99 red painted motorcycles, although Karl Marx would have complained about the inequality and probably would have insisted on everyone getting the same kind of red painted motorcycle or nobody should have even a bicycle, but the problem is that these vagabonding billions are used as a tool to influence the productive economy by sheer financial power. By this, and the size (many times of a normal state's budget), it becomes a tool for political blackmailing. If an elected politician does not dance to the tunes of the owners of such "assets" any Scrooge Mc Duck will withdraw his billions and trillions and by this potentially create a financial crisis. This has happened in the past decades a few times, while Mexico, Russia and East Asia had been worst effected but the threat is well and alive in the EU as well as even Jean Claude Trichet, the ECB president, has warned in an interview with the Financial Times. And, the EU Commission under President Barroso unlike any previous commission continues to throw sand into the eyes of the citizens by claiming that funds being 'freed' due to deregulation would be 're-invested' and by this create growth and ultimately jobs badly needed. This is, of course, the most cynical myth as it is evident that 4/5 of the newly accumulated wealth is derived from interests, funds managing financial instruments as well as speculations of which even European Central Bank President Jean-Claude Trichet at the Davos meetings spoke of "potentially unstable conditions" and that "there is now such creativity of new and very sophisticated financial instruments ... that we don't know fully where the risks are located." Frightening to think that the chief financial officer of the world's largest currency has to admit that he has no clue what is going on: "We are trying to understand what is going on but it is a big, big challenge." Trichet is quoted by the Financial Times on 29th January 2007. Well, one could help him. If he stopped listening to the representatives of the shareholders and instead studied thoroughly the EUROSTAT news releases he could know that a growth rate of less than 2% can not justify double digit profit rates unless someone went stealing. In the name of globalisation the Jedi Riders seeking to maximise shareholder values at whatever it takes bribe and blackmail by sheer financial power elected governments and parliaments and EU commissioners to push through a neo-liberal agenda which allows them to steal social and health care standards, pensions and unemployment benefits, educational and cultural diversity. The priorities are no longer set by governments and elected representatives of the public but by financial conglomerates no one can control. As public awareness has risen in the past 2 years to such an extent that even at that time German chancellor Gerhard Schröder, usually a friend of big business and shareholders, felt inclined to at least verbally vow to shut these money spinners down, knowing of course, that he would be stopped by the EU institutions which hold up the free movement of capital as well as free financial market principles, the European parliament also made a move to end the madness. Too many citizens who work hard started to ask why some mega rich are allowed to generate income from only multiplying numbers and zeroes without even putting some of their blood and sweat into this magic accumulation of wealth. After all, every Euro that is created by either real production or virtual reality money does represent purchasing power, in other words, someone has to work physically to produce a good that can be purchased. One does of course not smell which Euro has been generated out of a genuine production and which one has been derived from a casino table. The van den Burg report in a version that won't change anything at all although some of the rhetoric reads as if one wanted to criticise the various financial casino products bearing these exorbitant returns on investments. The report, however, concluded that a regulation of the financial market as such would reduce competitiveness of the EU's financial markets. On the other hand, one should ask why the largest internal market of the industrialised world with some 476 million more or less rich Europeans, should compete with the Bahamas, Panama, or any other off shore centre in regards to who has the bigger playground? As everything else is possible to regulate and is in many cases over-regulated from the size of an apple as well as the shape of a banana, it is hard to believe that parasitic financial 'products' can not be eliminated and accumulation of wealth be reduced to where production is happening, namely in small and medium sized entrepreneurships (SMEs) and producing industries.

The Blackmailing of a Government

◆

EU Commission lacking clear Environmental Position

July 2007

"There is one law for the rich, one for the poor" the famous Irish singer Christy Moore was singing in the 1980ies and today this line takes a different meaning.

The government of *Taosiaech* Bertie Ahern, the Irish minister-president who had been re-elected in May for a third consecutive term in office is confronted with mounting pressure. First of all, the Taosieach's personal finances came under investigation in a decade-long tribunal investigating slush fund scandals of the late minister-president Charles Haughey under which Bertie Ahern had served as an party executive handling finances and later as finance minister. Although the story broke during the election campaign it had hardly any effect on the outcome. Ireland was enjoying the most incredibly economic boom and although it transpired that it had been kind of artificially created by banks handing out mortgages of up to 120%, car- and consumer loans not seldom at interest rates below the rates such banks were refinancing themselves at the ECB and that soon payback-time would come, the Irish electorate wouldn't change horses during the race. Inflation is up again at more than 5%, partly resulting from the building boom. In the wake of a looming world wide financial crisis having to do with the over-valuation of property and with the EU Commission bugging everyone with their 'Climate Change' hype it can only be seen as a wise move by the *Fionna Fail*—Green government to initiate the changeover of the economy to "become a leading force in the drive of alternative energy" (Taoiseach Ahern). One would love to believe it and to rub ones eyes and say, that yes, there was at least one government throughout the EU, the government on "Green Emerald

Island", which did not get it all wrong and let the nuclear industry have a revival like in Eastern and Central Europe. Unfortunately, dreams are dreams and if they weren't the honourable campaign of environmentalists as well as local residents who can hardly be seen as NIMBY's (Not in My Back Yard) protesters as even the Taoiseach had to admit as they have good, scientific, reason to criticise the planned on shore pipeline construction in County Mayo, Ireland, would not have become necessary. The "Shell-to-Sea"—campaign has suffered another set-back as a high court decision ruled that the camp of the protesters was illegal and was "interfering with the environment" although the protestors had made sure that they had proper mobile septic tanks and would not leave any fast food wrapping around. These people usually don't eat junk-food anyhow. Coincidentally, just weeks ago a study found that some 80% of the green island was polluted. No wonder as the Irish still have a very lax attitude when it comes to environmental issues. Also, one could argue, that the exploration plant and pipeline no matter how nicely they will be painted will disrupt the wildlife and will have an magnificent impact on the environment. The sudden worries of the Mayo County Council officials and judges who followed their argumentation on how bad the impact the camp of protestors had on the ecology of this special part of the coastline appear to be a bit hypocritical, but that's how politics is. It also doesn't speak for the authorities that the "independent study" to prove that the plant as well as the pipeline was safe had been carried out by a UK based company who just recently had been made responsible for having endorsed a pipeline in Scotland which when it burst killed a family of four, two parents and two children. And, the role of the Irish government is more than dubious as in March 2005 the Minister for Communications, Marine and Natural Resources, Noel Dempsey, had the guts to present an "independent" Quantified Risk Assessment study conducted by the UK based British Pipeline Agency, which attested the proposed pipeline being safe. It later emerged that British Pipeline Agency was jointly owned by Shell and British Petroleum.

So what is at stake? Let's have a look at the facts: The "Corrib" gas field is a reserve of natural gas situated 80km off the West Coast of County Mayo containing an estimated 6–11 trillion cubic feet of natural gas. Today's market value would be some 50 billion €. And, who owns "Corrib Gas"? The largest stakeholder is Shell (45%), followed by StatOil (36.5%) and Marathon (18.5%). The Republic of Ireland: 0%.

The oil and gas is 100% owned by oil companies who find it. No royalties for Ireland. Shell and others only pay 25% corporation tax, in Norway it is 78%. All construction and exploration costs can be written off against tax.

"No other country in the world has given the oil company's such favourable terms" Mike Cunningham, a former StatOil director, said. So how is it possible that a government like the Irish Conservative-*Green* coalition who talks about putting everything behind *alternative energy concepts* and promises to clean up Ireland is allowing to have this major fossil fuel project materialise both, off- and on-shore undoubtedly bearing risks for environment as well as residents while not evening benefiting from it?

Well, the Ahern-government could argue that not to hold a stake in it could proof that one is not neither bias nor in favour of fossil fuels at all, but only naïve people would believe that. The more realistic approach would be to question the personal involvement of government officials since the oil and gas field had been discovered. In the late 1980's and early 1990's energy minister Ray Burke and at that time Finance Minister Bertie Ahern changed the terms governing oil and gas in favour of the oil companies. The terms cut tax rates and surrendered state control of oil and gas.

Mr Burke was later found to have received a number of corrupt payments during the late 1980s. In 2004 he pleaded guilty to charges of making false tax returns. The interim report of the Flood Tribunal in September 2002 found that Mr Burke had received a number of corrupt payments. The Taoiseach, Bertie Ahern, himself has gotten into the limelight of financial investigations lately as he had also received numerous inexplicable payments. This is the same man who had no problem saying that he found it alright to sign blanc checks for the late Charles Haughey, the infamous minister-president who had been at the centre of a decade long slush funds investigations.

It is, of course, questionable how sovereign a government headed by people who have their own finances not in order and for that reason accept that some dubious 'businessmen' are paying for their 'legal costs' (Ahern) in reality is. So, what could the Irish government, whether corrupted or not, do?

In 2006 the Russian government forced Shell to renegotiate a deal where they snapped up gas and oil reserves as the SU collapsed. The question, however is, whether the Irish government would be supported in anything like that or even a pull-out by the EU Commission.

It of course should be debatable why one should explore further oil and gas fields if at the same time José Manuel Barroso (JMB) is bugging us with his "climate change" talk since the beginning of the year. On the other hand, all the usual suspects, i.e. the US, Russia, Norway and even Denmark are currently staking their claims at the North Pole, now that most of the ice that used to cover it is gone. Polar bears are drowning as they have to swim ever farer to feed themselves and find a shell to rest on. And, farmers in Greenland are planting broccoli in the valleys from where the glaciers had retracted in recent years. The problem of the polar bears is that they don't like broccoli. The same is about to happen in Antarctica as well as the glaciers are crying icebergs into the oceans. Will the multinational oil mafia head for the Antarctic convergence once the ice has gone and laid bare the natural resources of Penguin-land? We can very well anticipate some guy in the White House tell us that the penguins were harbouring some dangerous al Qaeda terrorist and may be the president will link some of the hurricanes the US are suffering from to those terrorists and say "whoever is responsible for Hurricane Hillary, we will track them down and bring them to justice" while opening the fire on the poor penguins in order to make them surrender the natural resources of Antarctica?

The only valid question in this game would be: Why is Ireland not participating or at least benefiting from the Corrib Gas and Oil exploration?

And, the EU commission's position? They have none to offer other than that it was not for them to interfere with business as this would be bad for the economy, so it will be left to the environmentalists on Emerald island to tell the multinationals what the sights of the times are.

Back in the 1970's Dessie O'Malley planned to build a nuclear reactor in Carnsore. A popular campaign by ordinary people saw this plan dropped despite the Irish government's support for it.

Trichet's accountancy tricks

✦

ECB President defends monetary policy in EP
EU Commissioner Almunia: "Citizens not satisfied"

July 2007

ECB President Jean-Claude Trichet defended his decisions to raise the base rate of the Euro in the European Parliament on Wednesday citing the highest growth rate in the Euro-zone since 2000 despite high oil prices. The expansion of the Euro-zone economies had been 2.9% in 2006 compared to 1.5% in 2005. Inflation was close to 2% in 2006 and in the first half of 2007 just below 2%, the ECP president said. This is, of course, generally good news, one would say, but Jean-Claude Juncker, Luxembourg's Prime Minister and president of the Euro-Group, said that wage moderation usually demanded from workers and ordinary employees should also be executed by companies who awash their top management with millions. Citizens who "work from dawn to dust don't understand why they only get the peanuts while others were earning a fortune relatively easy" Juncker warned. Here the vigilant minister-president of Luxembourg almost sounded like a leftist fundamentalist just to laud a moment later the French president's proposals for structural reform. Tricky: just a day before Nicolas Sarkozy had laid open a business friendly concept of his government granting tax relief to major corporations while compensating the state's budget by an increase of direct consumer taxes and levies, in other words: another revival of the neo-classical model. This has not only proven to be disastrous in terms of domestic demand in Germany (-5.6% in the first half of 2007) but also finds less and less acceptance among citizens across Europe. In Germany, the Euro-zones biggest economy, 68 % of the population said in an opinion poll conducted by FORSA for the first

German TV, that the so called *Aufschwung* (up-swing) was bypassing them. And, even EU Economic & Monetary Affairs Commissioner Joaquin Almunia, usually getting indulgent on the "economic good times" admitted that he was "concerned by the fact that many citizens don't show great satisfaction about the Euro although there were good growth rates, less inflation and 2 million new jobs been created across the Euro-zone."

Well, let's apply the reality—check: The phenomenal growth Trichet is celebrating can mainly be seen in Germany, but obviously it doesn't even reach the 'normal' people there. Or can it really be called "economic good times" (Almunia) when in Germany, supposedly the Euro-zone's biggest and richest country children become a poverty risk and are in many cases not fed well as the major German TV stations ZDF and ARD reported in *Kontraste* and *Frontal 21*? Some schoolchildren have to starve, so the line of the news report goes. € 2.70 for food per day per child does not pay for a warm meal in Germany. In France, growth rates had throughout the last years been more consistent and stable than in Germany, averaging 2.7% while Germany was in recession, but, France is about to change this, as President Sarkozy announced on Tuesday in Brussels that he would overhaul the economic system which was too traditional. Maybe, but who says that all old traditions are bad? So far, France had lived quite well with these traditions, at least better than those countries who applied the neo-classical tools.

And, in the new member states the double digit growth rates can hardly be explained by a shrinking industrial and agricultural production but rather by an unprecedented consumer confidence, meaning that the Eastern Europeans which during the time when a barbaric border had divided Europe had been longing to get Western European goodies out of parcels sent by their generous relatives from West Germany, are all going on a shopping spree. Communism promised to get us all we need. Capitalism promises that we will need all we will get.

Like in 1989 when the Berlin Wall came down one can observe nowadays Romanians and Bulgarians, like the Hungarians and other new members who joined in 2004, to storm the shopping malls and emptying the shelves of the Western European, mostly German, retailers: real (Germany), praktiker (Germany), metro (Germany), Obi (Germany), Auchan (France), Metro (Germany), Lidl (Germany), Tesco (UK), Match (France), plus (Germany), dm (Germany), Baumax (Germany), Media Markt (Germany), Penny (Germany). The tragedy is that the German *Aufschwung* is exclusively relying on export. At the same time wages for the last two years in Germany decline. Not only the net wages but also the nominal figure. Employers cite the competition from Eastern Europe where labour costs are significantly lower. An unhealthy spiral leading downwards. The standard for employees will not be raised in Eastern Europe but lowered in the West. The best people in Eastern Europe may expect is to have their industries be taken over by a Western European company which will downsize it to the minimum and negotiate new contracts with the staff that has not been laid off yet. The double digit growth rates in the new member states almost exclusively relate to the growth in retail business, not production. The question how the Eastern European's consumption will be paid for when the economic tide retracts and leaves unemployment and high personal consumer debts and insolvencies behind, should be raised. But, maybe the EU Commission has further expansions on it's mind by this deferring the collapse further. Like in a chain letter system, also this will eventually reach it's limits, let's say for the time being at the Chinese border.

Traditionally, German industries had suffered from an expansion crisis. That being solved now since the Eastern European countries had to surrender their industries by privatisation that in many cases leads to de-industrialisation one had also observed in the case of the former socialist East German Democratic Republic when it was conquered by the West German industries in 1990, let's the CEO's and shareholders of the German major corporations send one cork after the other into the orbit when opening champagne bottle over champagne bottle with every DAX and EUROSTOXX gain reported.

In regards to the lower inflation rate one should add that overall the figure is correct, however, prices have fallen significantly in the so called "long lasting goods" sector such as electronic goods, pc's, audiovisual products, washing machines and cars (which can not be sold because of an ever decreasing domestic demand in Germany due to declining wages). The prices for goods collected in the food basket are not following this trend at all. Tomatoes, broccoli, fruits and anything freshly produced bear huge price increases, in some sectors double digits. As one doesn't buy a car or PC as frequently as one buys food, the "felt inflation" is indeed much higher than the nominal price increases. Almunia and Trichet surely are aware of this so they should rather not play the dumb who is surprised by the citizens who are not as grateful for the Euro as they say they expect we should be. And, last but not least, the 2 million jobs created in the Euro-zone in 2006 under the so called "Flexicurity" Agenda of EU Commissioner Vladimir Spidla are low paid (even though they bear a minimum of social protection). Two Thirds of the jobs are with so called 'recruitment agencies' who make a fortune on the back of the employees as in the majority of the cases these "new jobs" have replaced contracts having been governed by tariffs once negotiated by unions, a fact many people have looked through as a strategy by employers who wanted to lower standards as well as labour costs by threatening with redundancies. A positive side effect for the employers in Euro-Land is that this development not only makes it easier to hire and fire an ever more flexible workforce but also avoid future redundancy payments by simply shutting down a recruitment agency. Commissioner Almunia could know why citizens become increasingly disenfranchised with an economic system that does not let them benefit from "economic good times". Jean-Claude Juncker, although praising Sarkozy for his announcements to commit to exactly same neo-classical model, has said it clearly: Don't pay only peanuts!

Heiligendamm follow-up

✦

German undercover policeman not prosecuted

August 2007

The violence that erupted out of the blue towards the end of the peaceful Anti-G8 protest around the Heiligendamm summit has been provoked by several German undercover police officers of the "Kavala" special force who had been "accompanying" the protest marches and also had been infiltrating the camps of the anti globalisation activists, the German Spiegel Magazine reported on occasion of the release of a statement by the prosecutor's office saying that the file has been closed as there were no witnesses be found to the incidents. The accusations against the "agent provocateur", a police officer wearing civil clothes alike the ones worn by some of the protesters, to have thrown stones at the Heiligendamm security fence were dropped without the accused being charged with any offences. He had, according to several accounts, actively encouraged protesters to attack his uniformed colleagues by throwing poles and rocks. Since his behaviour had risen suspicion among the genuine activists he had been handed over by protesters and members of the defence attorney's emergency stand-by team who protected the undercover police officer from being attacked. The German police's special unit protecting the G 8 summit, "Kavala" had for some time denied that there had been undercover agents or even agent provocateurs but later had to admit that this was not the truth. The violence had erupted when a police car was attacked by a few men who had dressed like "black bloc"—autonomous protestors who are usually described by mainstream media as "notorious violent" troublemakers. The pictures went around the globe. What the media didn't show was that the police car, once all windows had been smashed slowly drove away.

The full video was later shown on "You tube" (http://www.youtube.com/watch?v=yDqThVpu1AM) and revealed that the whole attack had been a set-up.

It did, however, create justification for the German police to use water canons against the predominantly peaceful protesters provoking further violence. German Interior Minister Wolfgang Schäuble in the wake of the G 8 summit had introduced a series of harsh security measures from taking scent of potentially violent protesters to office raids of political movements like ATTACK and organisations helping refugees but also journalists being critical of the course the German government was pursuing when using the federal armed forces for the first time internally, a move creating a major dispute among the political class in Germany as it was seen as a departure of post war Germany's constitutional commitment not to use the *Bundeswehr* other than for defending Germany soil against aggression from outside. Schäuble repeatedly made the case that terrorism was an attack on the constitution from inside and that some of the anti-globalisation action groups were potentially harbouring violent terrorists.

IV.

Warshipped:
EU 'peace' missions

EP: Fuel to the Fire

◆

Darfur: Read between the Lions!

Showdown between China & „The West" at the Horn of Africa

July 2007

The European Parliament's Vice President Josep Borrell made an appeal to have the severe humanitarian crisis in the refugee camps in Sudan be brought under control by an international force with a clear mandate. At present, there are so called UMNIS forces from the Organisation of the African Union which are, Borrell said "not effective although the EU had financed the mission by some 400 million Euros per month". The Sudanese government, the Vice President of the EP said, had been "helpful and cooperative". The effectiveness of the OAU troops, however, was "at stake" Borrell emphasised and called for an investigation into the use of the funds sent by the European Union under the "Development Aid" Program of the EU and which do not even reach the troops. Wages of "peacekeeping OAU soldiers have not been paid for some months" he added. The UN's hybrid force which shall bear a stricter mandate was still many months away, the EP's vice president said while some 2.5 million people were starving and couldn't return to their villages as even a Nigerian OAU colonel confirmed that inside the camp he was a soldier but outside the camp a preacher. At the same time it has become evident that China was secretly financing some of the Islamic rebel groups which are aligned with the Sudanese government. Mr. Borrell said that while there was no clear evidence one for such direct involvement one should also speak with the Chinese government. The fact that the Darfur Crisis is more a show down of neo-colonialism between China and "the West" has been fed by the "Darfur Conference" held in Paris two weeks ago as President Nicolas Sarkozy had called for "repressive measurements" against the Sudanese government if they did "not cooperate". 'Humanitarian' NGO's and some UN experts had called in adverts published in the French daily Libération for putting the oil resources of Sudan under international control. This may explain why the Sudanese government will never agree to an international "peace force". China will also react nervous as it is the biggest buyer of Sudanese oil and block a decision which would effectively get the West into a better position when it comes to the exploitation of the resources. The Chinese special envoy for Sudan Liu Guijin rejected at the Paris conference that the government in Khartum was using army and militias to slaughter civilians. According to Guijin the Sudanese government actively tried to improve the humanitarian situation. This of course is seen different in the delegation of the European Parliament. Mr. Borrell said that people in the refugee camps had almost no food and soon also no more water and medical aid as the work of aid groups and NGO's were hindered by the ongoing fighting which also was fuelled by the Sudanese governments inability to create any kind of stability.

The Chinese magazine "China business" instead said in it's May edition (25.5.2007) clearly what in reality the issue was about: "Darfur: forget about the killings, there is oil." According to this article there was (since the Iraq invasion) a new cold war between China and the US over the control of the oil resources and that in Chad and Sudan the two countries were rivals.

In 2006 Sudan was the fourth largest oil exporter for China which buys 80% of the oil produced in Southern Sudan. China's oil concession in South Sudan concerns block 6 which directly borders with Darfur. After the Sudanese government had announced in 2005 that there was also oil found in South Darfur, all of a sudden rebel groups financed from abroad popped up and stirred the conflict. "China Business" accuses the US to prepare an intervention by NATO after a failed OAU mission that was deliberately give a weak mandate. The reason for the UN hybrid force's delay along with the disappearing EU funds which do not reach the OAU troops and by this further undermines their commitment can be seen as creating a justification for such robust intervention—all in the good and honourable aim to rescue innocent lives. European corporations are already sitting on the sidelines once the secession of Sudan has been manifested: The German Thyssen-Krupp Group along with other major European industries who through the European Roundtable of Industrialists (ERT) for quite some time lobbied the EU Commission to secure their bid on the Darfur region expects some 8 billion Euros in revenues from investments into the region according to the German financial daily *Handelsblatt* commenting on the German Bundeswehr's new *Weissbuch* in which the new "international character of the German forces' task" is laid out. One of the goals openly mentioned in the *Weissbuch* shall be to secure the "free and unhindered world trade, securing of the transport corridors as well as a stabile energy subsistence". The European Parliament once more engaged in throwing sand into the citizen's eyes by excluding such analysis from it's honourable initiatives to rescue human life.

Also in other aspects one can see how interests clash: China with it's double digit growth rates of the recent years has developed a certain hunger for natural resources. But, our "first world", the G 7 plus Russia and others are still dependent on the resources of so called "developing countries" as well. A neo-colonialism can be observed. It does not come along much nicer than a hundred years ago and it kills as much people. The natural resources of Africa are now in the centre of the interest of both, China as well as "The West".

Chinese metal resources imports 20 times more than in the early nineties. This new hunger for natural resources lets China concentrate on exactly those parts of the world, especially in Africa, which 'The West' has ignored for quite some time. The leaders of the 'Communist People's Republic' can not afford to become moralistic when talking about securing natural resources. Human rights always had played a different role in China, but one should not forget that the capitalistic West has also cooperated with fascist dictatorships in Chile, Paraguay and Argentina. Western politicians always want to forget this part when criticising China or Russia. China instead focuses pragmatically on what it needs to enhance it's rapid industrialisation. Chinese companies supported by the regime in Beijing find what they look for in exactly those countries outcast by a hypocritical 'Western World', namely in Iran, Sudan or Saddam's Iraq but also in Africa.

The prices for natural resources had risen by some 80% between 2003 and 2006, the price for oil doubled within the same time period. (Hamburger Weltwirtschaftsarchiv HWWA).

Tin, Iron Ore, Nickel and Cadmium as well as steel 'only' tripled but some other metals are traded for 6 times of what they had been in 2003. In poor countries, this has led to an incredible wave of theft of iron cables, any kind of appliances, even gullies were not save anymore. The German industry like most of the other European countries can not rely on any supply of such resources from domestic markets so it is vital to secure such in other countries.

German chairman of the Industrialists Federation *Bund Deutscher Industrie (BDI)*, Jürgen Thumann, pointed out at the "Natural Resources Congress" held in Berlin at the end of March that "Securing natural resources means securing the future." According to Mr Thumann it was vital that the German federal government founded an intra-ministerial committee of economical—, foreign- and defence specialists who should debate all resources related issues with representatives of the various industries. And, German chancellor Angela Merkel assured him of her full support: "You understood the signals of the time. Regarding the supply with natural resources the German industries should no longer be left alone. You will get what you need, namely a forum in which you can present your wishes and network with the political leadership."

One could sense that things have changed when India and China visited the G 8 in Heiligendamm last month. Usually, the noble club of the rich world and Russia doesn't allow onlookers when it comes together to conspire to find a common strategy on how to use the tools of the international organisations such as WTO, IMF and World bank on pushing through market liberalisations and to major multinationals favourable terms in GATT and Doha Round, but the leaders of the *Western Free World* along with the owners of the industries in the "first world" have understood that so called emerging economies also have their bid on the natural resources. Growth wise and soon by sheer economic power as well one should rather speak of 2-PLUS-8—Talks.

The strategy applied by the *Western free democracies* these days is simple: One has to spot a training camp for terrorists or even Mr. Ibn Ladn personally and can cite the necessity to protect against further Sept.11—attacks and bomb the place, like the US did it over Christmas last year and this years' Easter holiday, once more killing many civilians.

No one knows whether al Qaeda really has a base somewhere but the speculation about such alone justifies military interventions these days, at least when oil is discovered in the particular region.

Sudan's president Omar Hassan al Baschir felt safe by having asked Mr. bin Ladn to go elsewhere, so he was not pleased to hear that his country again was suspected to harbour terrorists. He, who had looked into every corner of his country and even in the drawers of his desk could not find a single al Qaeda terrorist but, of course, some rebel groups sponsored by whoever in the international community who gave him some headache forcing his government to defend the territorial integrity of Sudan. The "Darfur-humanitarian-crisis" loomed prompting the EU to call for an international peace-keeping force. Russia rejected this outright as "the presence of foreign troops like in Afghanistan as well as Iraq could worsen the conflict in West-Sudan" the Russian vice foreign minister Alexander Sultanan emphasised at the UN Human Rights council in Geneva just before Christmas last year. And, Sudanese president al-Baschir reiterated that the deployment of interventional forces by the UN was only an attempt to "re-colonise" Africa. His statements are usually not widely broadcast in the free western democracies. One prefers to show military running after children who starve in the desert. A *humanitarian crisis,* it appears, is initiated whenever it is opportune, i.e. when one found oil in Sudan or needs a strategic base for the next *Woild War* starting from Somalia. Then, of course, one doesn't want to have the main rival, The *Peoples' Republic of* China, have a foot in exactly that door one is about to shoot the lock off. And, also China is well prepared as Chinese companies have (supported by the government in Beijing) closed contracts with three quarters of the African countries and offered a debt relief of 1.3 billion US Dollars to 30 countries in which some 700 Chinese companies are active. And, last but not least, in Sudan alone are 4,000 Chinese 'civil' security personnel stationed to protect the pipeline owned by the Chinese National Petroleum Company (CNPC). Any questions?

Warshipped

◆

EU takes up arms

January 2008

Whereas the US never had a problem to speak openly about pursuing it's economic interests, the EU so far had been hiding behind humanitarian missions containing a touch of selfless "peace-keeping" because it's citizens wouldn't like to hear that their political leadership engage in neo-colonial behaviour. Americans don't have a psychological problem with that. US citizens are not against waging a war, they are against loosing one. Europeans, Germans especially, don't like to think of their governments to pursue economic interests of their industries. They prefer, especially if they are Green-Pacifists, to hide behind all kinds of excuses such as the necessity to "prevent Auschwitz from happening again" (Joseph Fischer, former German foreign minister) by finding *humanitarian* reasons for their military engagement. They worship their holy cows until they slaughter them cluster bomb by cluster bomb. The credo that troops in Afghanistan are "helping" the impoverished population and are welcomed by the war-torn people needs to be up-held. Unfortunately, main stream media does not report that since it's occupation in 2002 some 82 billion US Dollars had been spent for the military engagement but only 7 billion Dollars for development aid in Afghanistan.

Showdown between China & "the West" in Sudan

The priority seems to be military not aid. At present, 14,000 German soldiers are serving in 5 regions[1] which according to the German *Bundeswehr's Weissbuch* shall emphasise the "international character of the federal armed forces". One of the major goals described in this official document are "securing the unhindered

---

1. Handelsblatt 14th October 2006

world trade" as well as "protecting transport corridors and a stable energy supply". In Southern Sudan, the next project of the "EU human right warriors", the German Thyssen-Krupp Group was given the assurance by SPLM rebels operating in Southern Sudan to be allowed to build the 8 billion Euros worth infrastructure for the oil exportation after the successful secession from the country's North through which all oil export so far has been conducted. The Southern Sudanese rebels have pledged to pay for building said infrastructure by oil revenues. UMNIS troops shall guarantee stability of the region and by this manifest the secession. The government in Khartum reacted by waging a barbaric civil war. At the same time the People's Republic of China whose companies are already exploiting the Block B oilfield in Southern Sudan, bordering with Darfur, openly support the so called "Islamic Courts". Moreover, there are more than 5,000 'private' Chinese security personnel stationed in order to "protect" the oil operations. As nothing in China is really private, one could also speak of an army occupying this part of the country. As a humanitarian crisis loomed troops from EU countries are getting ready to "help". Like in the crisis culminating in Ruanda in 1994 the pre-text is European made: Back then, it was France which financed the Ruandian army bringing it from 10,000 to 300,000 soldiers who slaughtered a million civilians in a few weeks only while blocking UN troops and even during the beginning of the fighting delivered weapons to the Hutu Militias who also received support from the US government of William J. Clinton who saw a chance to push back French influence in the region.

Another proxy war as the international arms race is in full swing

And, in Congo the slaughtering between two groups evidently is a proxy war between Europe and the US who try to win bids in the licensing process of criminal privatisation campaigns in the mining sectors of the country. International major players are fighting over the licenses while the European public is distracted by mainstream media who focus on the question whether the elections are held "democratically" in a country which is about to be torn apart by rivalling groups. And, as the US is not even trying to hide their support for Sunnite rebels in Iraq as these are fighting with weapons delivered by the US against al-Qaeda and other radical "Islamic" groups[2] the EU doesn't see any reason to behave more modest but also invests into arms. In 2007 the expenditure for armament had

---

2.   Handelsblatt 12th June 2007

reached a record high topping the 900 billion Euros of 2006[3] which was already 3.5% more than in 2005 letting the expenditure for armament rise by 37% in the past ten years (137 Euros per capita of the world's population). The US alone had spent 400 billion Euros in 2006, China 37.1 billion for arms in 2006. Since 2002 the total arms exports have risen by 50% internationally, mostly from the US, followed by Russia and Germany (the latter doubling it's arms export since 2005). This may explain why armament plays a major role in the EU treaty: like in the draft 'constitution', the member states are obliged to "gradually improve their military abilities". Article I-40 makes it obligatory for the members of the EU to buy more and more weapons, even those we once were told had to be taken away from a man like Saddam Hussein because they were too dangerous. We, the European Union, will, of course, only buy those chemical, biological and nuclear weapons in order not to use them. In case that was true, a few bags of cement should do but we are told that we might have to use these in case we are attacked.

Lisbon treaty: obligation to increase "defence" budgets

Article III-212 of the Constitution goes even further. It calls for an "European Institution for Armament, Military Science and Improvement of Military Abilities". Until now the defence budgets have been varying a lot from 0.75% of the GDP in Ireland to 1.5% in Germany, 2.5% in France, 2.7% in Great-Britain and unbelievable 4.91 % in Greece. The US nowadays spends 3.03% of it's GDP on arms. With the creation of the European Agency for Armament the control of the arms race will be out of reach of the EU parliament or even the European Court of Justice, not to speak of national parliaments which until the new treaty will become effective always had a say in this aspect. According to the treaty's Article III-205 the European parliament will only have the right to be notified and consulted in this regard. It will only be the EU council, the governments of the member states so to speak, which will have power over the budget and the Agency for Armament according to Article III-207. Not even the Bush regime in the US has the sole power over how much the oil industry wants to spend on their adventures in the Middle East. Another red flag can be seen in the fact that the new treaty calls for a steady increase of the defence budget while it is clear that the military-industrial complex of Germany, France, Great-Britain and Italy,

---

3.   Handelsblatt 12th June 2007

especially the Airbus conglomerate, will benefit from this giving Bush a reason to verbally attack this development and citing illegal contributions by governments. While Bush was leashing out against Airbus and the fact that by government subsidies of EU member states an unfair competition advantage was granted to the passenger planes of Airbus which threaten Boeing. This itself is hypocritical as the US government clearly sponsors their military-industrial complex during their "War on Terror". A significant amount of the US' defence budget goes directly to Boeing which not only builds passenger planes.

Not only are the strategic consequences of an arms race and military rivalry with the US dangerous and unhealthy for world peace but someone simply has to pay for it and we can well imagine who it will be: the taxpayer in all member states. At the same time the ruling class as well as their political establishment and media never get tired to tell us that not the impertinent theft of the state's money by the multinational corporations and their shareholders by means of the neo-liberal tax reforms implied are responsible for the empty pockets of the state but the exploding social expenditure, which is, of course, a lie. The neo-liberal logic of Merkel, Brown and Sarkozy demands that tax payer's money is pumped into armament. For this, we unfortunately still have funds.

V.

The August 11th —Dossier

After 1989 only the world's major corporations and banks behaved in exactly the way Karl Marx 150 years earlier has said they would. And, before him, Adam Smith had postulated: Make moral your business. The only question is that if that had ever worked why has there been a Karl Marx, then?!

It is said that Socialists didn't handle their own arithmetic well.
In the neo-liberal digital capitalism the major players seem to think that it is sufficient to be able to count from Zero to One.

Out of Ginnheim

25th August 2007

Everything back to normal, one could think when one watches TV or opens daily papers these days. Has there been something in the mid of the summer? 11th of August? What was it again? Is the German Bundesbank in Frankfurt-Ginnheim happy? Hasn't it all somehow worked out in the end when the next door—ECB which is modelled on the Bundesbank flooded the market? Ah, yes, there were troubles on the financial markets which had been kicked off by the overvalued real estate market in the U.S. Now, three weeks later it is almost completely out of the news. Even the headlines of financial papers read as if nothing had happened. The truth is, that the whole collapse which in 1987 like in 1997 has been brought under control this time is once more only postponed. In 2000 it was imminent and in 2001 just two days before the September 11—attacks the headlines across the US from the San Francisco Chronicle to the New York Times read: "Bush worried about economy and boy he has reason to". The U.S. economy had overheated for 5 years during the Clinton administration and the recession every columnist still called a 'slow down' had been felt already in the last months of Clinton's presidency. The events around 11th September 2001 also provided for a market cleansing while some clever businessmen were able to bet on those stocks which were rising, like the military industrial complex as well as the airlines and oil industry corporations listed in the DOW JONES, while the e-business listings of the NASDAQ sharply declined. In a way, September 11 made US investors shift their capital back into production. The bubble created during the e-business boom of the nineties didn't burst entirely at once but also led to some market cleansing: ENRON and WorldCom were the biggest ones and although it had been common practice in all of the market, these two scandals stand for how sick the whole system was and is. The cash that became available quickly found a new boom it could initiate: the property boom. And, this time the US markets were clever enough to spread the risk by inviting international investors from overseas, many German banks but also East Asian and Japanese institutional investors who were willingly participating in driving the money spinning wheel. Former German chancellor Gerhard Schröder's *"Neue Markt"* had collapsed and those who hadn't lost all went into the US' hedge funds. The beauty of capitalism is that it gives everyone the feeling of being allowed to participate and that if one was clever enough to put money on the right horse one could be lucky and become rich. Socialism relied on the hard working and sweating masses. Capitalism relies on masses who try hard to find ways to avoid hard work and sweat. In Germany there are some 750,000 High Net Worth Individuals (HiNWI's as Merrill Lynch calls them) who each own some 3 million Euros, a third of which they hold in cash, investment bonds, stocks and shares. The mainstream media obviously is currently trying to calm these masses down because if they become nervous the effects could be felt in an accelerated way. The next richer class of the Ultra High Net Worth Individuals (UHiNWI'S) wouldn't love to see the HiNWI's withdraw the snow they need to keep the snowball from falling apart before it becomes an avalanche that goes downhill. The Europeans as well as the South East Asians and Japanese have all participated in the unhealthy US bubble building. The Germans, especially, can not see the US decline as their export would be at stake. The Eurozone's powerhouse is confronted with a constantly declining domestic demand (-5.6% growth in retail trade in 2007 so far) so the whole saga about the German *Aufschwung* becomes fisherman's yarn if the US market does not call for BMW's, Volkswagen and Mercedes Benz anymore. It shows what the German up-swing really was: a bubble relying on a bubble in the US. Well, one can, of course, solve the problem by applying the same logic: fill one hole with another. That's why Jean Claude Trichet called all shots in the week of August 11. The reason why he could do so by flooding the financial markets on one day tender basis with some 250 billion Euros without causing inflation is to be seen in the fact that those funds never reach the man in the street but only the banks and by this do their job right where they are needed most: on the financial market. That this self-financing closed system like the space station ISS can repair it's own failure has to do with it's isolation. As long as gold cover was underlying the amount of circulating cash this would have been impossible. On the other hand: many of the problems we have today with these vagabonding bubbles would not exist either.

That's why Bernanke can play cool and let it be sorted out by the markets themselves.

How sovereign are the Central Banks?

✦

Bin Ladn at the Roulette table?

Who holds the asset backed commercial papers?

September 2007

Osama bin Ladn, the man who apparently is in a midlife crisis as he was dying his beard and eyebrows before announcing to join the anti—globalization and environmental movement came under a new suspicion. Would he rather than bombing his way through to Fort Knox knock soon on the doors of England's most prestigious banks and demand to be paid out billions over billions for asset backed commercial paper of which no one at present knows who these are held by. These market IOU's nobody much wants has to be rolled over at volume of up to 130 million Dollars. On 17th September alone commercial papers amounting to 48 billion US Dollars have to be refinanced. Two days later it will be another 18 billion, then towards the end of the months on the 21st, 25th and 27th of September it will each be just less than 10 billion so probably still manageable, but then at the beginning of October it will be almost 60 billion and another 28 billion Dollars in Mid October. The Problem is that the market for these ABCP Programs has dried out by now during the past weeks after August 11. Many emitters of such papers have already prematurely reverted to the credit guarantees issued by banks. In simple terms it is as follows: If a bank grants a loan it credits the creditor's account with such. The creditor will make use of the loan facility by transferring it to a third party at another bank, in this case to the owner of an expiring Commercial Paper. For the lending bank it means that her account at the central bank will be debited with that amount. As this account can not be overdrawn for not only one night, lets the bank refinance itself through the money market. In other words, the bank has to take out a loan from other banks who have received money from such transactions. That's the money market loan. Normally, this should not pose a problem as the banks who have received money through such transactions are happily lending it out on the money market to the other banks from whom they will be paid an interest. At the moment this system does not work anymore as the banks started to mistrust each other and therefore are more than reluctant to lend each other money. This accumulation of super-fluous money which is not as usual brought back into the cycle has led to the huge unbalances of the money market what is reflected by the heavily changing rates for daily money market interests. The interest rate for Euros has at some stage hit 4.6% whereas the ECB would like to see it rather at 4%. That's why the ECB offered on last week's Thursday a quick tender of 42 billion Euros which effectively led to the daily interest in this week be much lower than the 4% base rate of the ECB, namely at 3.1% which the ECB also doesn't want. That's why Trichet offered on Tuesday of this week superfluous liquidity to be "parked" at the ECB for one day. And today (Thursday 13th Sept. 2007) Jean-Claude Trichet offered additional funds on a 3-months-basis which shall have the effect to lower the interest rate for 3-month—loans granted between the banks which this week still has been unnaturally high at 4.7%. While Trichet is doing his best to level out the huge imbalances of the market, the Bank of England is under fire from the money market bankers for playing cool. Even the German Frankfurter Allge-meine Zeitung[1] noted that neither the FED nor the ECB are truly sovereign in this crisis. Politically they are independent, the conservative paper writes, but not so from the financial markets. "The financial crisis more and more becomes a test for the independence of the central banks—the independence from the financial markets, not politics." Here one can see a different behaviour in Great-Britain. The London City is paralysed as their central bank, the Bank of England, is remarkably stoic in its monetary policy during the crisis.

"Asset backed commercial paper is rolling back off every day and the banks are taking more and more on to their balance sheets which is using up capital." Paul Mortimer-Lee, global head of Market economics at BNP Paribas is quoted by the Sunday Times[2]. According to this expert it is "both, a liquidity and a capital cri-sis".

Investment bankers are of course nervous, especially since the central bankers in England played cool in reacting to the crisis. The Bank of England's Executive Director for Markets, Paul Tucker, the probable next governor of the Bank of

---

1.   FAZ 11th September 2007
2.   „Emergency Injection" by David Smith & Grant Ringshaw 09 September 2007

England, has made it clear that he believes that it is not the bank's job to protect "unwise lenders from the consequences of their past decisions."

The Bank of England's decision to only inject some 4.4 billion Pounds Sterling each week over a 3 weeks period was heavily criticised David Smith wrote in the Sunday Times[3] but he also makes the point that while "the money markets are in turmoil … the 'real' economy remains strong". David Smith writes that one could be "forgiven to think we have two parallel economic universes. The one in which the ordinary consumers live is doing well." The reason why it is not without an impact what happens on the financial markets our colleague gives himself by quoting David Kern, economic advisor to the British Chambers of Commerce who outlines that the "increase in cost and reduction of availability of money to business is quite dangerous" and may further slow down the prospect for the British economy.

That would raise the question why the real economy should suffer at all from the irresponsible gambling on the casino tables of the virtual reality and why one should be depending on these Jedi Rider's luck in betting on the right horses and not like in reality hand out tokens rather than real coins and notes.

---

3.   09 September 2007

Ja, Ja, Jakuzzi

◆

Power-Cut in the Bubble-Bath

Buy it, strip it, scrap it, sell it

September 26th 2007

The man with the full grey beard once more dipped the feather in the little ink pot before he wrote the last sentence of an economic conclusion. "It may happen that an amount of lending capital is made available which only to the degree that it stands in diametrical opposition to the relation of productive accumulation." The old man leaned back in his armchair and took a deep breath, something we all should do these days in order to brace ourselves for what is yet to come. In spring this year this planet's financial institutions were bathing in lukewarm Dollars raining down on them. Deutsche Bank AG chairman Josef Ackermann uncorked one champagne bottle after the other when celebrating the best quarterly profit report in the history of the most traditional and powerful German bank. Profit had risen by another 30% while the return on investment was prompting Deutsche Bank Ag shareholders to send champagne—corks into orbit: 41%!!! This record return was largely owed to the investment bankers of the institution who accounted for three quarters of the pre-tax earnings. The classical business of a bank, to take deposits and hand out loans became marginalised. The bulk of the newly accumulated wealth was resulting from gambling with stocks, IOU commercial papers, derivatives as well as the consultancy business the bank offers for takeovers, mergers and acquisitions, which is easily earned money for the bankers. In the first six months of 2007 the volume of corporate acquisitions worldwide had reached an unprecedented 2.7 trillion US Dollars which had been triggered by so called 'Private-Equity Firms' whose business idea can be described as buying more or less healthy enterprises on loan basis while later imposing the loan onto the balance sheet of the company which by then will be downsized to the absolute minimum. The remaining managers usually are bribed by phenomenal pay increases in order to sweeten the later-over deal for them and make them be extraordinarily efficient when it comes to lean management and redundancy negotiations. Once that has successfully been completed and 'superfluous' workforce been laid off the company is usually handed over to the next Jedi Rider or Private Equity-Shark who even makes profit in case the company goes bankrupt as the tax dumping competition between states allows for a leveraged buy-out (LBO) as the lucrative return on 'investment' usually stems from tax incentives granted to financial investors and their credit financed bonanzas.

The amount of such transactions had doubled between 2005 and 2006 while the banks were queuing to finance the Private Equity firms. An average of 80% of the transaction volume is usually financed by cheap loans. The transactions became larger and larger, the prices more and more exclusive. The most spectacular coup was, indeed, the takeover of 80% of the shares of Chrysler through the US financial investment house Cerberus for 12 billion Dollars. Also ready to go were 50 billion Dollar deals for the energy supplier TXU, the Canadian telecommunications concern Bell Canada or the Credit Card handling company First Data. All of a sudden nothing works anymore. Even 'done deals' of which the ink under the contracts is not dry yet like in the case of the US American soft drink producer Schweppes for 8 billion Pounds Sterling through a consortium of Private Equity Firms has been put on ice. And, also the Chrysler-deal only evaded a last-minute fiasco by the owner, Daimler, to grant Cerberus a loan. This absurdity illustrates how desperate Daimler was to get rid off Chrysler which goes down in the history of take-over's as one of the greatest miss speculations. No bank finances any of these snowball systems anymore as banks these days keep any Dollar they can get their hands on and put it into their own pocket before they even think of lending money that cheaply. Even banks only lend money to each other at a higher interest rate which had led to the central banks to inject billions of Dollars and Euros into the money market in order to avert a run to the banks like it happened already in the 'North Rock'—case in the UK last week. Since a while, banks whose traditional business should be to hand out loans and by this play a vital role in the 'real' economy by giving liquidity to manufacturers, retailers, inventors and producers have been eager to spread if not sell their risk to others. Major banks, especially, only want to act as mediators for credit arrangements rather than taking on the risk. The most celebrated innovation in the financial world has been the so called "Asset Backed Securities" (ABS) which are consisting of presumably somehow guaranteed packages of loans. One version of the ABS are the so called "Residential Mortgage Backed Securities" (RMBS). In the latter loans of different risk categories are pooled meaning not only the interest and terms for re-payment of principle are important but also and very much so the potential default rate. Like the buyer of stock has a claim on the profit share of the company that has issued the stocks and shares the holder of the RMBS claims a portion of the interest and principal payment. One does, of course not know, how big the portion of the bad loans is that is hidden in the pool. The trick the financial institutions employed in order to spread the risk when placing the RMBS on the financial market was simple: they split them into 3 (or, in some cases, more) trenches while each of these trenches are dealing with the potential default in different ways. The lowest ranking trench is the one bearing the highest risk and can only be sold with a high withholding for the high risk meaning that it can only be sold at a low rate. If, in the end, there are less defaults than expected in such trench, it helps the holder of the RMBS to make an extraordinary profit. Therefore, these RMBS trenches of the lowest ranking bearing the highest potential risk provide for becoming the ideal tender (although it should rather be called token) for the playground of the Hedge Funds whose 'speciality' is lying in obtaining the maximum profit out of risky investments. The second trench, referred to as 'Mezzanine', already appears a bit less risky as it is only affected by losses if there is an over—proportional default rate. The top end of the trenches instead is aimed at showing a high level of security although the package is still full of high-risk level loans but because it's profits are only affected if there are extraordinary and so to say 'historic' dimensions of losses been reached, are rated by rating agencies like Fitch, Standard & Poor's, or Moody's, with AAA. In other words, these dubious trenches were given the same rating as real solid, state guaranteed bonds, such as US treasury bonds or the German government's *Bundesschatzbriefe*. By the mere construction of the RMBS the wildfire-like creation of virtual funds had not been brought to it's worst yet. The next trick employed was to have 100 of such mortgage-bundles to be bundled into another package, the so called 'Collateralised Debt Obligations' (CDO), which were brought to the market by pretty much the same method. This vehicle was sellable outside the bourse and was sold in Europe, but also in China and Australia as a 'low risk—high profit' (if ever anything license to print money had existed like such, how would it be explainable to make 30–40% profits annually when the growth rates were tumbling around and below 2%?! One should ask whether the sellers but also the buyers were sane!) euphorically by bank conduits, hedge funds but also pension funds and insurance companies. The trick of the double guaranteed and diversified trenches allowed it to transform high-risk loans into a seemingly safe investment. And, because these dubious CDOs appeared to be almost risk free, the demand never eased off and by selling more and more of them allowed the banks to issue more high risk loans without really taking on any risk themselves. That really was the license to print money. In the past weeks it has become clear that the AAA ratings of the CDOs have been as fraudulently manipulated as the ratings of WORLDCOM, ENRON and Parmalat, who also just until very short before their collapse had received the best ratings. Because the rating agencies are not neutral observers of the scene but earn their money with such manipulations one shouldn't be too surprised about their behaviour. The EU Commission's rating agency bashing is a bit hypocritical to say the least. Rather than deregulating the EU Commission had rather *regulated* the financial market and protected the citizens of the EU from the brutal consequences of loosing their pensions, savings, investments, jobs and houses.

The global deregulation—wave has lead to today's capitalism showing a similar beauty as the capitalism of the first half of the twentieth century which had burnt itself in an unprecedented way into the collective memory of everyone who had survived two world wars, holocaust and Atomic bombs. There are definitely memories one doesn't want to revive.

PS: Back to the old man in his small working class house somewhere in England: "On the other hand, the trading with these promissory notes that are largely created solely for the fabrication of other of such I-Owe-You papers which may create the image of solid businesses bearing interest and providing for a good return on investment even though such is already resulting from defrauded lenders or producers will let it appear prosperous, indicating phenomenal growth rates. In fact these returns will always let the business appear especially then remarkably healthy when the crash is imminent" the old man wrote with his ink pen and sighed in relief as he closed the third volume of the book which should become one of the most famous and most hated standard work in economics. Now, the man rubbed his long beard and thought about a title. Keep it simple he said to himself as he scribbled down only two words: "Das Kapital". Then, Karl Marx turned down the oil lamp and got ready for going to bed.

US & EU in same raft, not boat

◆

Why the EU can't kiss the US bubbles good bye—yet

October 2007

The Euro's performance over the past few years is stronger than the US dollar's. So one could ask why the EU let's itself be drawn into the US' financial malaise. One reason certainly is that the European financial corporations and banks wanted to participate in the North American *Wirtschaftswunder* and although they knew how hollow that "e-business boom" was Clinton & Gore had initiated being followed by the Bush administration's *un-*"real" estate—hype which at least had the collateral be made from chipboard and cardboard built houses that are frequently been blown away by hurricane after hurricane, underlying it, rather than the hot air Clinton and Gore tried to sell tin by tin, was. No, the European banks and institutional investors are not victims at all as they knew exactly what they were doing when going to bed with the wrong bride. Another reason can be seen in the fact that the Eurozone's economic 'powerhouses', France, Italy and Germany, especially, rely on their export to the US and like a delicatessen retailer would hate to have their most loyal customer choke from eating Caviar by the spoon and drown in a bath of Champagne even if he hasn't paid his tap for a while.

Everybody knew, nobody said

The problem is that although August 11th has disappeared from the headlines, the problems have not vanished. Our financial system suffers from structural problems and by putting it off for a few weeks, months or even a year or so, doesn't mean that it doesn't persists. The nasty thing about cancer is that it is spreading further even under the surface. It can only do so because it eats the body from inside. Most analysts and economic journalists knew and have frequently expressed that they were concerned about the overvaluation of stocks, shares and real estate but wouldn't speak about the consequences.

Donors sought

Nevertheless, the Europeans together with the South East Asians as well as emerging economies such as China and India but also the so called Third World were financing the US' bubble. Even the poorest African state which holds Dollar reserves in a way co-finances the US. Time would be ripe for the Europeans to kiss the ailing US financial markets "Good Bye" but the two blocs are too much interdependently linked, with the Eurozone's "powerhouses", Germany, France and Italy, relying on the export to the US. Germany, especially, has all it's *Aufschwung* the much celebrated 'up-swing' at stake as the domestic demand collapses (-5.6% in the first quarter of 2007) due to shrinking wages. On the other hand, there has been, since German unification, a shift in politics between the US and Germany making it hard for diplomats to make it look as if everything was 'normal'. It is not only the German's unwillingness to participate in the Iraq (ad-) venture. The Schröder government had no problem engaging in NATO's 78-day-bombing campaign against Serbia in the bid over Kosovo or declaring their "unlimited solidarity" with the US after the September 11—attacks. The reason why Schröder did not stand shoulder on shoulder with Anthony Blair and George W. Bush in the crack down on Saddam has not been a suddenly discovered pacifism but the fact that the German industries had sold their oil business to Shell and BP at the beginning of the nineties. Instead, the German energy consortia engaged heavily in the Russian gas business making Gerhard Schröder's move to become a board member of GAZPROM after he handed over the office to chancellor Angela Merkel look like a logic though in it's openness not predictable step.

Even now, under Angela Merkel, Germany will take a more careful approach when it comes to dealing with Iran. First of all, the German federal government has bonded by some 128 billion Euros the German industries' Iran—business with so called *Hermes Garantien*. And, although one doesn't want to see the Americans and British go and shoot at the lock of the door one has a foot in, there has been a sudden shift away from that position as Dresdner Bank AG and Deutsche Bank AG after intense pressure from Washington who threatened[1]

---

1.   Spiegel online 23rd August 2007

quite openly German bank CEOs that their institutions might face consequences when trading in the U.S. gave up their Iran business following in this move most of the other European financial institutions who like Credit Suisse, UBS, ABN Amro and those from France and Great-Britain had ceased from providing the Dollar Clearing since last year. This means that international trade, especially when selling oil, for the Mullah regime can not be cleared in US-Dollars anymore. This does neither hurt the Ahmadinejad—government as the whole international trading has since March 2007 been switched over to Euro and other currencies, nor the German banks who only reported double digit Dollar clearing as a result from the creation of the Iranian bourse for oil (IOB) which is exclusively operating in Euros anyhow.

The Iranian Bourse for Oil

The US are currently suffering from a situation worse than under Ronald Reagan whose government had to deal with a double deficit which lead to the devaluation of the Dollar. Bush (in all fairness, the grounds had been laid by Clinton's and Gore's e-business bubbles) had managed to create a triple deficit for the first time in US history. The triple deficit (budget—, performance- and trade deficit) of today will lead to depression, especially since the U.S. Dollar is now rivalled by the EURO. The US is missing a 400-billion-dollar-influx of foreign capital annually if its leaders want to compensate the performance deficit of 6.5 per cent of the GNP. George W. Bush has understood and so he took the gun and went out for hunting as the US economy needs 2 billion USD per day to make good on the triple deficit. However, when you are seen going out with your gun in the mornings it is not good to be seen coming home at night without a bear hanging over your shoulder. In Bush's case it is even worse: someone else is about to get the fur of the bear. Usually all oil sales are traded in US Dollars. That may explain why Bush has just recently asked for further 50 billion US Dollars from Congress for the military engagement. It doesn't look like a troop withdrawal but rather like the preparation for another war.

As all economies are still dependent on oil the currency exchange rates are decisive and technically the US Federal Reserve has huge obligations towards the whole world as oil exports are paid in by US Dollars. Only because the US Dollar has been (for the past 100 years when the Pound Sterling vacated that position which marked a departure from British rule in many parts of the world) *the* world leading currency the size of such obligations didn't matter. The US could print as much money as they wanted and was needed because they were the only country which was to pay for its foreign debt by the own currency. Any other country doing so would have choked by inflation. Now, with the Euro rivalling the US Dollar openly it becomes increasingly difficult for the US to level out the imbalances. In order to do so there would be only two options: either the US would have to increase it's export by approximately 22% or devalue the Dollar by 43% towards the Euro. That's why the Dollar is trailing the Euro for quite some time already. However, the Europeans, the solely export relying German industries especially, have no interest in the Dollar further declining.

Under these circumstances war appears to be the only way out as the US can not really become onlookers for the new Iranian Oil Bourse (IOB) in the Persian Gulf which trades oil sales in Euros only. Of course, one will say, the turn over doesn't amount to much but one stands at the beginning and even if it is a more symbolic thing to happen, it tells a story. US Dollars and also the Pound Sterling are left out of the noble club. Maybe that's another explanation why those countries are so eager to go to war. And maybe that's why Germany is so reluctant. Like almost 75 years ago, when German capital was standing against American capital it is now the Euro versus the Dollar.

Historically—
Who is to be blamed for the US' decline?

◆

Written by Ralph T. Niemeyer[1]
in July 2003

The American 'Dream'

When Alan Greenspan decided to lower the interest rate on 3rd January, 2001, NASDAQ rose the very same day by 14.2 per cent, and produced the biggest-ever growth within a day in its history. The value of all American stocks rose by 700 billion U.S. dollars. But only a day later, everything was back to normal again. And when Greenspan lowered interest rates again by half a per cent each time in February and March of the same year, the stocks even tumbled into a kind of mini-recession, and nothing like a phenomenal growth could be stimulated. Greenspan's tools were loosing their power.

In the last decade of the twentieth century, the amount of money invested daily on international markets reached an unprecedented and unbelievable four trillion U.S. dollars. Even more is spent every day in trading stocks and derivatives. The *Hausse* of the nineties has solely been financed by these virtual funds, which although not backed by economic output or real production, indeed have some significant influence on the real economy. In monetary theory, this would

---

1.   An extract from Ralph T. Niemeyer's book "Waiting for the new Führer—The German Euro Apartheid" published in July 2003. The book is still available at http://www.amazon.com/Waiting-New-F%25fchrer-German-Euro-Apartheid/dp/0595295525/ref=sr_1_4?ie=UTF8&s=books&qid=1201370259&sr=1-4 as well as in Barnes & Noble's shops and online: http://search.barnesandnoble.com/booksearch/isbnInquiry.asp?z=y&EAN=9780595295524&itm=1

mean direct and permanent inflation. The fact that this is not the case proves that inflation itself is not primarily a monetary problem but one of real fights about ownership and distribution of wealth.

Excessive creation of virtual funds does not necessarily lead to a significant increase in demand for goods and services. Whether or not this unreal and excessive creation of virtual funds really affects the demand for products and goods as well as services depends on who has access to this virtual liquidity.

The main problem in regards to the effects of interest policy is not that the base rate decides whether investments are made and jobs created, but who has access to liquidity and at which terms and conditions, and of course, who controls this access. Usually, this is governed by credit committees of the banks, but it is also controlled by the distribution mechanisms of the financial markets. The latter is less and less influenced by the central bank's interest policy.

For more than five years the United States was seen as the success model, accounting for an annual growth of nearly five per cent, decreasing unemployment, booming stock markets, price stability and even stunning budget surpluses. It appeared as if all economic goals were perfectly met. Clinton and Greenspan made possible what European governments were struggling with over the past decades. But was that really so?

Yes, during the term of the two Clinton-administrations more than 8 million jobs were created, but without any health insurance, pension plans or Social Security. Millions of Americans hold down at least two, if not three, of these six-dollars-an-hour jobs, more than forty-one million Americans have no health insurance, while Social Security benefits (under Clinton & Gore) were limited to a total of five years per capita, and limited to one time in a life. On the other hand, the number of inmates in U.S. federal or state prisons quadrupled since 1977. And since autumn, 2000, growth stagnated and major retailers employing over 38,000 people went bankrupt. Car dealers were sitting on new models, manufacturers like General Motors (15,000) and Daimler-Chrysler (26,000) reduced their work force significantly. Two years before (1999), hundreds of thousands of jobs in the productive industries were cut, and even e-business and internet companies issued so-called "profit warnings", although these should rather be called 'losses'. Stocks were falling. Dow Jones finished its worst year since 1981, loosing 6.2 per cent in 2000. NASDAQ within one year lost 3000 billion U.S.-dollars. A sharp recession has followed despite Greenspan's attempts to fuel the economy by lowering the interest rate again and again. It's of no relevance for the financial markets if these figures represent only virtual economic potential, and are not linked in any way to real production of goods or services.

Important in this regard is the growing gulf between rich and poor in the United States. The differences have never been larger. Between 1977 and 1999 the net income of the richest one per cent of the society has risen by more than 115 per cent (clear of inflation), while the top 5 per cent of Americans could account for 43 per cent, and shocking for a rich nation like the United States, the net income of the bottom 5 per cent of society shrank by 9 per cent below the level of 1977. The middle class of three fifths of U.S. citizens were able to increase their purchasing power only by mere 8 per cent in twenty-two years, despite ten years of incredible boom.

A study of the Economic Policy Institute acknowledged "… that the gap between the pay of average U.S. workers and that of top corporate executives has exploded …" In 1980 it was a ratio of 42:1, but just before the September 11—attacks it was 419:1.[2]

This planet's real economic growth between 1980 and 2000 rose by 80 per cent, while the market capitalisation at the world's stock markets generated a virtual growth of 1032 per cent during the same time. The Dow Jones alone, for instance, grew by an unreal 200 per cent between 1995 and 2000; some internet and new technology titles reached several thousands of percentages of growth, while the relationship between share prices and profit seemed to be irrelevant. Stocks were bought in order to sell these at a higher rate, and as long as everyone believed in it the system worked. In 1996 Greenspan warned of an irrationalism, which was only at its beginning.

The American boom of the nineties was largely created by the rise in private consumption, but with the real net income diverging as laid out above, it was possible to finance such increased consumption only on credit-bases, or by consumer loans, credit cards, mortgages and personal loans which led to the American people being indebted as they had never been before. Private bankruptcy cases piled up in the courts, families were destroyed, and social existence became a privilege. On the other hand, it isn't realistic to dream that the boom could have been initiated by increased spending and consumption by the top 5 per cent of American society, as those very rich would not eat more, or buy more washing machines or many more cars than they already have. Middle class Americans were not able to initiate this boom by their share (+8 per cent consumer spending in twenty-two years) without financing or re-financing it by personal loans. So what justified the enormous virtual growth reflected by the stock markets? Few real factors have to be taken into consideration: There have been, of course, some signif-

---

2.   All figures from International Herald Tribune 6th September 1999

icant changes in the world after the collapse of the Communist regimes in Eastern Europe and the Soviet Union. Opening of Eastern European markets for the major international corporations, access to resources and raw materials, privatisation, re-structuring, deregulation and industry-friendly tax reforms in Western countries as well as in the emerging markets in the former East generated a tremendous wealth in the western hemisphere.

Whenever the U.S. economy was in danger of getting stuck it was helped by an influx of cheap loans. And even stocks were accepted as underlying security, although these "collaterals" were heavily overvalued, but nevertheless served the only purpose: to buy new and more overvalued shares. The Hausse fed itself. This mechanism was well alive in the nineties, since the volume of loans of the stock exchange-registered investment banks and stock traders tripled between 1994 and 1999, and reached an unreal 278 billion dollars in March, 2000.

The trick employed by investment bankers was a simple one: refinanced by loans, the capital available for private but also institutional investors could operate hedge funds and derivatives. This new liquidity, as virtual and principally unlimited as it had been, fed the overheated stock market. This virtual and unreal financial bubble indeed had very real consequences on the actual and real economic cycles of production and consumption, and thus laid the ground for the 'American boom' in the nineties.

The mechanism employed created an enormous wealth for the top 20 per cent of American society. On the other side there was an increasing indebtedness, which also contributed to this boom, as it artificially and very short sighted created a purchasing power that will one day bounce back at the same pace rate at which the loans are called in by the banks. During the second half of the nineties, private debts of American households grew by 10 per cent annually and reached an unbelievable and very unhealthy 103 per cent of the real income in 1999.

One need not be an economist in order to conclude that this could not go on for long. The International Herald Tribune (IHT) noted on 6th September 1999 that "the gap between rich and poor in the U.S. widened to a record." This is the America Clinton and Gore (the latter likes to be seen as the 'inventor' of the internet) formed. The *Frankfurter Allgemeine Zeitung* (FAZ)[3] reported that "The U.S. economy becomes vulnerable" as the performance deficit rose to 4.5 per cent of the GDP, commercial debt accounted for 63 per cent of the GDP (in 1994 it had been 56 per cent), while loans taken out for purchasing stocks and shares amounted to 220 billion U.S. dollars in 1999, up from 126 billion USD in

---

3.   Frankfurter Allgemeine Zeitung (FAZ) 22nd May 2000

1997. The total amount (nominal value) of stocks in the U.S. exploded in the Clinton-Gore years to an all time high of 170 per cent of the GDP, three times higher than the *Activa* of the banks. Forty-five per cent of the population had invested in stocks, even if they did it by borrowing, over-borrowing and gambling with their pensions and retirement savings and homes.

According to the U.S. Department of Agriculture, more than 31 million Americans in 1999 were partly starving or at least had to worry about their next meal. More than 12 million children in the U.S. go to bed each night hungry.

The U.S. had to deal with a threat of a depression as serious as the great depression before the Second World War. In October, 2001, more than 700,000 Americans lost their jobs, sending the unemployment rate into orbit (within a month from 4.9% per cent to 5.4 per cent; in 2000 it was still at 3.9 per cent) hitting 7 per cent in spring, 2002. In the year 2001 alone more than two million Americans lost their jobs. Meanwhile, economic growth shrank by 0.4 per cent[4]. Although the U.S. economy was in recession, Americans consumed as never before. The performance deficit rose from 4 per cent of the GDP to up to 6 per cent. In order to finance this deficit the U.S. needed an influx of 2 billion U.S. dollars foreign investment per day. As this is highly unlikely, the devaluation of the dollar is inevitable. Until recently (2000) the deficit financing has been conducted by foreign direct investments and by selling stocks. Nowadays, (July 2003), 95 per cent are financed through bonds, which are the much more expensive way of doing it for the state. Because the interest on those bonds is relatively high, America will have more and more difficulties to pay off its debt.

According to Handelsblatt,[5] there would be only two options: either the dollar will devalue radically by at least 43 per cent, thus making American products incredibly cheap and trigger an export boom, or the foreign demand for U.S. products had to rise by 23 per cent if the dollar rebounded.

At present (2003), many American economists and analysts fear that the U.S. could experience the same malaise as Japan, which has not recovered since the bubble of financial and real estate markets burst at the end of the eighties. The collapse of the stock market in the U.S. led to a loss of 4,500 billion U.S. dollars in assets for U.S. investors.[6] Because of highly exaggerated profit expectations, many companies are highly indebted now, as they expanded tremendously and

---

4.   Handelsblatt 4th January 2002
5.   Handelsblatt 22nd February 2002
6.   Handelsblatt 15th July 2002

created over-capacities. Only two facts have so far prevented the worst: low interest rates enabled regular citizens to re-finance their loans and mortgages and consume the money they saved, and secondly, the rise in the real estate sector allowed them to access higher mortgages on their homes. Both effects are quite limited and can not be expanded indefinitely. Once interest rates only go up a tiny little bit, these will turn into bad loans and potentially trigger a tremendous turmoil.

The average American today (2003) is indebted by more than 105 per cent of his annual income. Fifteen per cent of the incomes are usually spent on interest and repayment of principal. With stocks falling, more than 80 million Americans lost 2000 billion dollars within weeks. A person who two years earlier invested 10,000 U.S. dollars in diversified stock funds only had 2,200 U.S. dollars in his portfolio in 2002. The overall economic data before 11th September, 2001, showed dramatic slowdowns: GNP shrank at pace rate, growth figures for 2001, previously expected to be 1.2 per cent, reached only 0.3 per cent. The trade balance also turned negative. In August, 2002, the trade deficit was 38.46 billion U.S. dollars, exports dropped by another 1.3 per cent, while imports steadily rose by 2 per cent.[7]

The double deficit of the Reagan years had led to the devaluation of the dollar. The triple deficit (budget, performance and trade deficits) of today (2003) will lead to depression, especially since the U.S. dollar is now rivalled by the EURO. The U.S. is missing a 400–billion-dollar-influx of foreign capital annually if its leaders want to compensate the performance deficit of 6.5 per cent of the GNP, to which it will climb by the end of this year (2003). Under these circumstances war appears to be the only way out.

The collapse of the American economy was predictable, and the events of 11th September, 2001, only accelerated the decline and in a way rescued the president-in-charge who gave a weak performance until he could declare a war, a war which NASDAQ did not want, as the shares were dwindling even faster. Dow Jones instead needed such a war, and the stocks of heavy industry, manufacturers and especially the oil industry grew at rapid pace.

---

7. Handelsblatt 21st October 2002

US' Fed deliberately departs from Greenspanology

September 2007

If there was an analogy that would serve the purpose of illustrating in comedy style what has happened last week in the headquarters of the Central banks of the leading economies one could say that while ECB president Jean-Claude Trichet had pulled up his sleeves and was soon to take off his neck tie turning all tabs to the left flooding the restraint financial markets with some 200 billion € on day-tender basis for 4,07%, and the Japanese central bankers had been climbing up Mount Fuji passing through the "forest of no return" where many suicide-aspirants commit Sayonara, were throwing Yen notes downhill, the chairman of the US's 'Federal Reserve', Ben Bernanke, had gone fishing. Jean-Claude Trichet on 6th September injected another 42.245 billion Euros as a quick tender with an average rate of 4.13% while all Bernanke did was to lower the Fed funds rate on 18th September by 50 points taking it down from 5.25% to 4.75% and a month later another 0.5%. The reason why Bernanke didn't do it right away in a knee-jerk reaction can be seen in the fact that he wanted to avoid a moral hazard and merely execute good anti-cyclical monetary policy as he was given a week earlier the perfect excuse with the employment's report "lowering expectations" while actually for the first time in 5 years jobs were lost. It simply looks better for Bernanke not be accused of bailing out improvident lenders to sub-prime borrowers but rather do something about the real economy which employs people.

A lot more at stake in Europe

The US's Fed only half heartedly tried to rescue the market with some 30 billions whereas the ECB did it at full scale and with much bigger volume. Obviously the German *Aufschwung* is at stake as even the EU Commission had adjusted it's growth forecast for 2007 down from 3% to 2.3% because of weaker than expected performances by the three major Eurozone economies, Germany,

France and Italy. Further 'adjustments' may be necessary, soon as the restrained financial markets will not put that easily money behind production for a while. Germany especially will be hit hard by the crisis as all it's up-swing had been leaning on export, most of it to the US. The domestic demand in Germany was already collapsing since the beginning of the year. Consumption went down by 5.6% in the first quarter of 2007 due to constantly declining wages in Germany.

But, there is a general change in strategy to be observed at the Federal Reserve Board. Alan Greenspan always fuelled by lowering interest rates even to the negative, but Ben Bernanke did so only very modestly, so there are new signals coming from the Fed. Even when only a few equity funds were in trouble, Greenspan lowered interest rates when during the South East Asian crisis in 1997 only two hedge funds were in trouble. They had been major ones, ok, but today the situation would also justify fuelling the market by lowering interest rates. At some stage the paradox became real: the interest turned negative. Technically it would mean that I had to pay a bank to accept the money of my piggy bank and had to pay my bankers interest. It could only be worse by not bringing the piggy bank to the bank at all as the negative interest resulted from the inflation being bigger than the nominal interest. Savings were eating themselves.

Greenspan helped create bubbles

All the cheap money Alan Greenspan had made available on the markets had the effect that huge bubbles were created. Today, one has to avoid that the foam is being presented at the cashier's desk. This would apparently lead to self—enhancing chain reactions. And: one shouldn't play domino on the deck of the Titanic. And, especially not if one had won a seat on one of the rare life rafts. European banks have participated in the equity bubble and logically are now suffering from having taken over risks their US counterparts had been clever enough to spread.

The cheap money financed all those mega mergers, fusions and takeovers. Now, it is payback time and the European banks are paying for their lust to eat from the poisoned cake of the US mortgage bubble. The US banks generally can only congratulate themselves as they have managed to spread the risk in a way that the Europeans are not able to take advantage from their crisis. The crash is felt both sides of the Atlantic and that may be the reason why Bernanke didn't see as much reason to intervene as his European counterpart Jean-Claude Trichet showed. He just does the bare minimum to keep the market afloat so that no one can say that he had not done something. But, it is clear that because of the world wide spread risk the US banks won't suffer from the turmoil to the extent they are responsible for creating it.

How to get a seat in the life raft

A lot of foam has been created. The unequal income distribution of the past years that had started with Clinton's e-business boom when NASDAQ grew by some 114 % in only one year while Dow Jones barely made it to some modest 0.5% of growth just before Sept. 11 did not result in an ever greater consumption as the rich class wouldn't eat and drink or even purchase any kind of goods in such a steadily increasing pace rate that the US' domestic demand could fully recover. And, the refinancing of consumption through mortgages is a quite limited scenario. It also leads to—de-saving, rather than saving.

Private equity funds are usually owned by those who helped create the bubble by handing out cheap money to the Jedi Riders: the banks (and by this the shareholders) themselves. The sympathy of the ordinary citizen with those may be limited, the only question as always is who will get a seat in the life raft and who not.

Psychologists @ work

◆

Useless "Analysts" & Rating Agencies

September 2007

The famous rating agencies, Standard & Poor's, Moody's and Fitch as well as the smartest "analysts" of investment banking institutions and major accountancy firms once more got it all wrong. None of them had offered a valid and in any way useful advice although it had been obvious that the hedge funds "industry" was facing big trouble.

What a good analyst ECB President Jean-Claude Trichet could be becomes clear when one recalls what he had told the participants of the World Economic Forum in Davos in January of this year when he warned of "potentially unstable conditions": that "there is now such creativity of new and very sophisticated financial instruments … that we don't know fully where the risks are located." Frightening to think that the chief financial officer of the world's largest currency has to admit that he has no clue what is going on: "We are trying to understand what is going on but it is a big, big challenge." Trichet is quoted by the Financial Times on 29th January 2007. The ECB president was right but obviously couldn't prevent it from happening. In the last weeks he was rolling up his sleeves and was busy pumping some 200 billion € on tender-basis into the financial market in order to prevent it from collapsing completely. In any case the damage was done as investors worldwide had received a wake up call and those who managed to save some of their funds for a while will be reluctant to put these into jeopardy again. A positive side-effect: at least no one will continue to debate the question whether wages shall partly be paid by offering shares to the workforce, a dreadful proposal that always plays a role in economic "good times" when major corporations want to reduce wage costs.

But how is it possible to make someone believe that while economic growth is less than 2% and rise of productivity around 2.5% on an annual basis profit increases of 30–40% per annum and more are possible? Well, it takes some well dressed "analyst" looking serious into the TV cameras to speak to the wider public of "stable market conditions", "'A' classifications by rating agencies" and "confident investors". A good deal of psychology is a part of the whole scenario as well. Granny, every housewife and even students who may have saved a few pennies knock their piggy banks and bring it to the banks as they want to participate in this miraculous money spinning fortune wheel. Some Gurus dominating the markets have their "analysts" spread the word and the masses follow them. But who are these "analysts" and rating agencies we trust? Do they create a market where there is none? Could be as once their clients have followed their advice, then the bubble starts to constantly grow, like a snowball system. And, whoever had gone where the snowball is going to run to first, will be able to earn the most. Like in the good old chain letter system we all played in school, the amount of people participating is somewhat limited and once one doesn't find anyone to sell a share for more money one has bought it for the miraculous perpetuum mobile all of a sudden needs some engine oil to smooth it's wheels. The Analyst's job is to not let the general public doubt that the system would survive the *tiny little crisis* although it has been clear by then that the peak has been reached. This is the moment the big investors go out of the market. Like when Deutsche Bank AG two weeks before August 11th called all shots and let Sear's Bank down by calling in the loans. Granny who still doesn't smell what is cooking continues to believe that smart analyst on TV who tells her that there were only "minor irritations". Analysts got a fine job. They can not be held responsible and they can not be controlled. If they fail to predict a crisis they claim that they are only publishing "opinions". Well, understatement may be chic but in reality those agencies, at least the major 3 rating agencies like (until the Arthur Anderson—Enron—World Com scandals) the "big Five" accountancy firms, have more power than any central banker of the FED, finance minister, US president or even Deutsche Bank AG who ironically just a week ago announced that legendary Ex-FED-chief Alan Greenspan joined the board of advisors, would ever have.

Two side notes:

Greenspan:

Another populist has spoken out when Alan Greenspan the long time chairman of the FED famous for his cryptic statements shredded the economics policy of the Bush administration while lauding the Clinton administration although most of the economic problems the Bush administrations had to deal with stemmed from the Clinton-Gore—administration's e-business boom. Before Bush declared one war after the other which Greenspan says had been over oil (in this analysis he is unbeatable!) the US economy was in bad shape because of the swollen bubbles Clinton's boom created. That the conservative White House financed the wars with deficit spending should be criticised but Alan Greenspan is not really credible in lecturing about the economic agenda of Bush & Cheney and it's flaws when one considers his own role in the 2003 rate cuts that led to the creation of the housing boom, the bubble after the e business bubble that are directly responsible for today's worldwide financial crisis.

Northern "Pebbles":

Brown: Economy which prior to the August 11th—financial crisis that peaked with the Bank of England preventing "Northern Rock" from being turned into a basket of a few pebbles, has been—other than in the Euro-zone—quite healthy, started to suffer from the market's downturn prompting the PM who was flirting with the option to call an election to legitimise his government to drop such plans like a hot potato as the opinion polls showed that although he could not be blamed directly for the financial crisis voters would not accept that Gordon Brown who as chancellor of the exchequer has been overseeing for 10 years the development on the financial markets had been hiding in the bushes. Public sentiment rather is that Brown could have come up with preventive legislation of the kind "Everybody's" Darling, the new chancellor of the exchequer, pulled out of the drawer of his desk in the aftermath of the run on *Northern Rock* suggesting a securitised mechanism to protect savings.

Audit, tax & laud yourself

September 2007

The big three rating agencies all have a certain tradition and by this reputation.

The history of the rating agencies goes back into the 19th century when the US railway companies were laying their tracks over the North American continent. Loans were required but the banks alone couldn't put it all on their shoulders. The companies issued bonds in order to raise funds. Henry Varnum Poor published in 1868 the "Manual of the Railroads of the United States" in which the equity investors would find information about the railway companies. In 1941 Poor's Publishing Company and Standard Statistics fused to become Standard & Poor's. John Moody founded his "Moody's Investors Service" in 1909 while John Fitch formed his "Fitch Ratings" in 1924 out of "Fitch Publishing Company".

The question is whether these firms rightfully can play the dumb or whether internally they do have much more sophisticated analysis at hand for let's say their most important clients. Otherwise it would hardly be explainable why the crash of the sub-prime mortgage market which had been at least predictable since 2004 as it was even written about here and there and that eventually had lead to the current crisis on the financial market had not been reflected in the "ratings" and "analysis" the smartest of the financial world made public. It could rather have to do with the fact that having certain information and knowledge about imminent crashes exclusively and sooner than others poses a clear advantage for some Ultra-High-Net-Worth-Individuals (as Merrill Lynch calls people like Soros) as well as institutional investors and shareholders. Like major banks, these privileged clients pull in their umbrellas right before it starts raining. Then, the "ratings" all others have trusted along with the "analysis" of really smart economists the masses of medium and small investors have followed like a guru all of a sudden are *adjusted*, in other words, the truth about the over-valued real estate market, stocks and shares, the tins full of hot "e-business"—air, "sub-prime lending"—bubbles and virtual reality casino tokens made from *financial instruments* such as derivatives gets out onto the streets. Medium and small investors loose,

but also SME company's who are relying on cash injections to enhance their productions are suffering. And, without a rating it is almost impossible to obtain
liquidity. In a way, the whole system of rating agencies and published analysis
invites manipulation and so far none of the agencies have laid open which exact
mechanism and scientific grounds their "opinions" are based on. They all hide
behind obscure mathematic formulas they do not want to lay bare so in a way it
stays unclear where Mathematics end and opinions begin to kick in. Even the
German Spiegel magazine criticised the lack of transparency. Given the nature of
the financial business that should rather be accurate and digital one would think
it can only let the observer be left astounded that once more all rating agencies,
major accountancy firms and analysts have so completely and on a large scale
failed to see the dangers which indeed had been foreseeable even without applying high mathematics but this may not have been in the interests of the most
powerful clients of such firms. EU Internal Market Commissioner Charles
McGreevy, once an accountant himself, had vowed at the beginning of this year
to enhance the accuracy of the accountancy firms by having them *voluntarily*
agree to a new code of practice which they would promise to adhere to. My question whether it would not be naïve to think that an accountancy firm which is
paid huge sums for doing an audit for a major corporation by exactly same is
potentially experiencing a conflict of interest and whether it would not rather be
required to control these major accountancy firms and rating agencies back then
was countered by the commissioner throwing back at me what kind of mega
bureaucracy I was dreaming of. Well, if that could prevent a financial turmoil
potentially forcing major economies worldwide into recession or even depression
while leading less advanced countries into deprivation and their populations into
starvation, one should consider to invest into such a controlling body. After all,
each member state entertains enough revenue commissioners to deal with millions of citizens so what's the problem with doing same for the major corporations, their shareholders, auditing companies, rating agencies and "analysts"?

A lot of Foam

◆

The Myths of EU growth rates

October 2007

The Spanish finance minister Pedro Solbes is anything but in a good mood these days. 'Spain is braced for pain as Germany slows down' the Financial Times at the end of September headlined quoting Solbes as saying that "a problem for Germany is ultimately a problem for all of us". That is, indeed so as Germany is Spain's biggest export market but as private consumption in Germany is on a sharp decline due to a constant decline of net wages less and less imports are made while Germany through it's major retailers Metro, Lidl and Aldi is exporting more than ever before. But, Germany is also the key source of capital market finance for Spain's 10 year economic boom, in which German savers funded Spanish property development. Construction, like in many other countries which celebrate a boom like Ireland, Malta and the new Eastern European member states who account for growth rates between 3 and 11%, is the only viable business apart from retail business which is also growing in these countries at rapid pace while the agricultural and industrial production declines sharply raising the question how this consumption can be financed in the long term. Joaquin Almunia, the EU Commissioner for Economic and Currency Affairs is not worried, he told me in April of this year. There was no problem with growth rates relying on retail business as long as the trade balance can be paid for, he emphasised. But, such growth rates are artificially created and the seeming good performance can not be repeated over and over again every year. The truth is that the construction business is only booming because homes and shopping centres are being financed by 100% leading to overpriced buildings built well beyond demand thus increasing inflation where it should be deflation. If there are more goods (in this case apartments and houses) available than there is demand, prices would fall. In Ireland house prices rose by 300% because like in stock markets the snowball system worked for a while quite well and although every Irish citizen today technically speaking has two houses, which are in most cases not paid for, the market is soaring by now. On top of that the GDP is 30% higher than the GNP, meaning that 30% more accumulated wealth leaves 'Emerald Island' than stays there. One would think that someone who has already to worry about financing two houses at home would rather not speculate with the risk to loose all, but the Irish who overnight felt rich were told by their mortgage brokers and bankers that it was okay to have a winter retreat for the dark, dump and dull days in November, so they collectively went house-hunting in Spain, South Africa, Bulgaria, Malta and other sunny locations. Mortgages are taken out and are secured by the houses back home in Ireland. The real estate stock of the 4.5 million people is valued at some 700 billion Euros whereas the GDP although it nicely grows at around 150 billion each year does not justify such valuations. Internal Market Commissioner Charly McCreevy, an accountant by profession and the former finance minister of Ireland who helped initiate the "Celtic Tiger" still sells it as a success model and unfortunately the list of bad examples becomes longer since the collapse of the internet, dotcom and e-business bubble could only be averted by moving the foam that has been created in the nineties was pumped into real estate. As there was not enough real estate available that could absorb the thousands of billions of liquidity a construction-hype lead to an artificially property boom that like in the virtual reality casinos of the stock markets could continue on a *perpetuum mobile*—basis although such neither in physics nor in the financial markets does exist. The latter only appears as if there is such thing like a self-feeding Hausse although it is rather a snowball system: As long as you find someone who is more stupid than yourself to buy these obligations, stocks or houses from you at an even more inflated price it may work, and there are, of course, some 7 billion people on this planet, and, if this is not enough, there may be extraterrestrials out there in the universe. Since the "inventor of the internet" as he wanted to be seen and in his time as Vice-President actively helping to create the dotcom-bubble resulting in the WORLDCOM, ENRON and Arthur Anderson scandals, Albert Gore received the Nobel Peace Prize for bugging us with 'Climate Change', it has become clear that the next bubble after the real estate markets collapsed will be the alternative energy—"Green DAX" which already is over-financed as THE GUARDIAN wrote on 27th September. But, where else should all the foam multiply itself for another few years?

The EU Commission currently seems to have concentrated on this kind of business as in most Euro-zone countries, except for Germany, the industrial production is stagnating or on the decline as the building and construction boom comes to an end. Pro cyclical developments are at hand. The banks face a significant default rate but won't loose out as they will write it off. As most balance sheets despite the constrained financial markets are still showing double digit profit rates it will just a bit of tinted port wine on the tax statements of the financial world once more socialising it's losses having the tax payer step in for the poor shareholder's value. Deutsche Bank AG has just a few months ago reported that while it's profit

Affected are not only Ireland, Spain and Malta but also Czech Republic, Hungary, Slovenia and Poland. Moreover, the business is mostly conducted by West European major corporations like STRABAG and ING who also receive the subsidies from Brussels to build up the infrastructure in the new member states. In case the markets go down, like in Ireland, recently, the bad loans, if not sold out to hedge funds, are written off by the banks, in other words, the tax payer jumps in and covers the miss speculation. The same is now about to happen in Spain but Pedro Solbes disagrees with critics who believe Spain is vulnerable on three counts: an overheated and overpriced real estate sector, the over-exposure of banks to that sector, and a large current account deficit which all has become symptomatic for what the EU Commission tries to sell in their PR campaigns and by their lobbyist-journalists as a model for economic success. The reality is different: In it's table headlined 'Europed together' the Financial Times on 27th September of this year gave the figures for the Euro-zone economy. According to the EUROSTAT figures Export from the Euro-zone to the UK is down from 19% in 1999 (the launch of the Euro) to just 15% in 2006 while the export from the 13 countries to the US had peaked in 1999 with 17% and now landed at 14% in 2006. In other figures the dream of a "economic good times" (Almunia) becomes a farce. The contribution to Euro-zone GDP growth between 2002 and 2006 points in all countries downwards except for Germany. Spain accounted for 22% of contribution of GDP growth in 2002. In 2006 it was only 12% with this year showing already another sharp decline. This may explain Mr. Solbes' headache. The "success story of Europe" (McCreevy), Ireland, managed to halve it's share in GDP growth from 4% down to 2%. The "Celtic Tiger" is weeping not roaring anymore. The Financial times call those economies "building and housing bubble junkies" and in this the colleagues are certainly right.

Newcomer Slovenia from 2% down to un-erotic 0%. What a great success story for a country which only joined the noble club in January of this year. Even during the time the country was part of Yugoslavia it had looked at a better economic performance. The only countries who perform better are France which was able to increase it's share of the cake by 1% up to 21% in 2006 but in 2007 is already on the decline building up a fast growing trade deficit. Germany alone was able to raise it's share of GDP growth in the Euro-zone from 17% to 27% in 2006 with further increases at hand in 2007 due to it's expansions into the East of Europe while the market at home in Germany is on a constant decline due to shrinking wages and a brutal regime of drastically reduced social benefits and pension cuts.

VI.

50 more years?

People's Congress?!

◆

1st Agora: European Parliament reaches out to "citizens"

October 2007

Agora is the place in Greek towns where more than 3000 years ago the polis dem-ocratically decided on all essential matters. There couldn't be a more direct par-ticipation of the people in the decisions of the community. Now, the European Parliament, well based on democratic principles and democratically elected as the European citizen's representation all of a sudden wishes to hold an "Agora" about the Reform Treaty which is bound to replace the draft "constitution" which although being negotiated by politicians, "outside experts", and NGOs under presiding reputable elder statesmen had fallen through in two referenda.

With this new instrument of a mega-hearing the European Parliament wishes to bridge the gap between politicians and civil society, the vice president of the EP, Gérard Onesta, explained. For two days the "representatives of the civil soci-ety" meet the representatives the European public has elected on 13 June 2004 for doing exactly same but not only for 2 days but rather five years. There can be no doubt that even the selection of the 640 "representatives of the civil society" has followed democratic principles as 11 committees of the European Parliament decided over whom to invite. Asked how it was made sure that not the over-whelming majority of the participants of the "Agora" were recruited from the 17,000 lobbyists in Brussels, Vice President Onesta replied that of course they did not invite the Polish plumber or the Sicilian social worker but rather the umbrella organisations of these. In other words: Non-Government Organisa-tions, NGOs. NGOs per se have a positive attribute as it suggests that they are neutral when it comes to political party partisanship and therefore can speak with a higher legitimacy. That the moral is not necessarily higher when NGOs act is proven by the fact that many of them have a long time ago understood how lobbying works and Lobbyists have learnt that it sounds better if one is a NGO rather than a consultancy or public relations firm. So the NGOs have a mandate to represent the "civil society" to discuss the reform treaty which governments try to impose onto the European citizens. Asked what the difference between the lobbyists and NGOs who meet the MEPs every day and those who are coming now to represent the "civil society" was, Vice President Onesta said that most of them have never been in Brussels before. Well, the European Parliament is a nice place to visit and the city of Brussels an attractive location for tourists. A few of the "representatives of civil society" had already arrived on Tuesday. In the evening a famous NGO of Germany, the consumer protection organisation *Deutscher Verbraucherschutz* held an informal gathering including canapés and champagne in the rooms of the restaurant in the European Parliament. A Press-attaché of the European Parliament, Jens Pottharst, admitted that only "selected journalists" had been invited. Four fully accredited journalists were not allowed to enter. Next door, another NGO executed a less strict policy when dealing with the media which in a way can also be seen as—of course unelected—representatives of the European public. It was the British Banker's Association, BBA, who at least let two English speaking white journalists in and have a chat with the bankers and their NGO's spokesperson. The other two, non-white, journalists from Algeria, were not welcome. This can be seen as symbolic as the European society is quite split at the moment, not only in regards to the reform treaty but also when it comes to social, cultural and religious exclusion. So today the first "Agora" shall debate the reform treaty which will be signed on 13th December in Lisbon. Gérard Onesta, who as vice president of the European Parliament was one of the initiators of the gathering explained that if a "document of a high quality" was the result of the discussions of the "representatives of the civil society" and the representatives of the citizens it would indeed have an impact which would be widely reflected in the media. Ah, here we journalists are all of a sudden welcome again: when it comes to distribute the acclamation of the reform treaty by this *Volksdeputiertenkongress* which is rather bearing reminiscence of Stalinist style "People's Congresses" just that in China or North Korea there are not that many visible NGOs. Today's "Agora" will probably produce a "quality outcome" as the Vice President wishes to see it. He didn't want to speculate at the press conference last week what would happen if the "representatives of the civil society" did not come to the conclusion that the reform treaty is in the best interest of the citizens. It wouldn't have an impact on the ratification of the treaty of Lisbon anyhow, as referenda can only be called by the governments of the individual member states. Anything else, would be too democratic, but a "positive result" as the President of the EU council, Portuguese Minister President Sokrates, hopes to see from the "Agora" will be welcome. The next "Agora" will be held in spring 2008 and it will be, guess what: "Climate Change"! Will they ask the "People's Congress" to vote in favour of nuclear plants and the "Green DAX"? And, if the one after that one will be about "Terrorism" our Islamic colleagues probably will be allowed to attend again.

The night of Lisbon

◆

Why the Coup d' État by the European Parliament became necessary

13th October 2007

I saw clear after I spent the night before the EU summit in Lisbon last week walking through the city, along the promenade at the EXPO '98 where the European heads of governments were to meet a few hours later, thinking about the EU and where it will go from here. Since I didn't manage to find a hotel room I was left walking around all night but then finally stretched out on a bench in the little park next to the conference centre. I dreamed of a beautiful lady, *Europa,* who had trouble with her husband, the EU. I was woken up at 6 by a few joggers. One of the faces looked familiar. It was Nicolas Sarkozy. The French president ran as if it was for his life. I slowly got up. What a strange dream, what a coincidence! I thought about the marriage of the EU with *Europa* again and why the majority of the citizens had mixed feelings about the EU. Like in a marriage only the naked truth counts. Unfortunately, the husband (the EU) is sending text-messages from the edge of the bed he shares with his lover (major multinationals) to his wife (*Europa)* telling her that he couldn't call right now because his meetings continued well beyond midnight. Now, it can't be called a mere coincidence that the European Parliament will vote this week about creating "EP TV". Who would be interested in it, one may wonder as opinion polls show that the citizens across the EU are yawning when being told about the European Parliament.

All totalitarian regimes tried to control the media and manipulate the thinking but never managed to do so over a longer period of time. In the EU the periods of time become smaller and smaller as the opinion polls show. The Eastern European Stalinist dictatorships had a centralised power, security and media but it didn't help them as the power of the supposedly free information channels from the West had been superior to suppression. The more the old Stalinists spread their lies on the 3 state controlled TV stations the less the people believed in the system. The beauty of the Western Free Democracies is that they allow a free media. It is now 300 TV channels who can tell us the same. A trick of the system is that everyone has to feel free and if he doesn't than he has to blame himself. In the Stalinist times everyone felt un-free but could blame someone else.

The Financial Times recently published[1] an opinion poll according to which only a quarter of the EU citizens of the five largest EU countries said that the EU had improved their lives. 44% instead saw a decline in their standard of living. But, leaving the EU is also not seen as an option. Only 22% think that this is a good option.

EU citizens are not only not really interested in EU affairs, but as the Financial Times found in another poll[2] are in their vast majority disenfranchised with the economic system which almost 70% seem to find not holding much in store for themselves. The majority of citizens asked across Europe also expressed concern that the EU could be in danger of copying the US' economic model. But this is exactly what the EU is already doing increasingly for the past few years and with signing the treaty of Lisbon into effect will even further enhance this kind of economic model. *Europa* when she was still a bride had no clue what husband she was about to get married to. He didn't play with an open hand and now as the cards are about to be laid onto the table, it is too late to just close the eyes and simply carry on. The marriage is at stake once the trust is gone. When a couple experiences such difficulties in their marriage they either divorce or they try it again. In the latter case it will only work if both sides speak openly and truthfully with each other. All facts need to be put onto the table. In the case of EU and *Europa* it would be necessary to explain to the bride why statistics were manipulated. The husband should admit that he wasn't able to hunt and bring home as much as he said he was for the past years.

The EU Commission's 'Creative' accounting

In the case of the EU it is the fact that the reported growth rates are manipulated. In order to do so, the EU's statistical office, EUROSTAT, was forced by the Barroso—Commission 3 years ago to introduce hedonic pricing, meaning that growth can be calculated in a very creative manner: a washing machine which ten years ago had let's say 10 programs today has 20. Under hedonic methods this

---

1.   Financial Times 14th July 2007
2.   Financial Times 26th September 2007

allows for an adjustment of the figures for quality improvement. Unfortunately, it doesn't mean that more washing machines have been produced and sold. It is easy for a statistical office to show impressive growth rates this way although in reality they are stagnating or even declining. Currently, the industrial production[3] was up by 1.2% in the Euro-zone and 0.9% in the EU27 excluding construction. But to know this is worth nothing unless the adjustments being made are laid open. Using the hedonic methods of pricing allow any manipulation Almunia may dream of. In construction, indeed, this is not possible and that's the reason why it is separated from the overall outlook. In the Euro-zone, construction increased by mere 0.4% in August compared with July[4], in the EU27 it was a stunning 1% with the largest increase in the new members Romania (+37%), Slovenia (+31.4%) and Poland (+14.8%) and the largest decreases in Sweden and Germany (-3%). The banks (usually all Western European) in the new member states like they have done it for some 13 years in Ireland financed and over-financed the building bubble so that massive inflation resulting from a self-feeding bubble is now threatening the standard of living of the majority of citizens in those countries. It won't help to tell the people that because of hedonic pricing the economic output were increasing. It is simply not true and the people feel it. The Euro-zone's GDP[5] was up by 0.3% (EU27 +0.5%) in the second quarter of 2007 and some 2.5% (EU 27: +2.8%) compared with the second quarter of 2006 but this is largely owed to the construction sector creating supply overtaking demand by bulk as well as the retail trade, but no real industrial growth. The statistical methods employed hide these facts very well.

The US did this for much longer already and much more excessively. In a way, not much growth has been happening in the US in the nineties. All Clinton & Gore created were dotcom bubbles which in the Bush years were wobbling into the real estate market which just recently collapsed. With the help of Al Gore's noble peace prize whatever has been left over from these bubbles will sweep into the green technology industries. All price indexes one finds in the US' Bureau of Economic Analysis in the NIPA (National Income and Product Account) tables about economic growth suggest that without the various adjustments like such for "quality improvements" there was not much of a real growth at all. Nevertheless, the prices were rising while the standard of living is constantly declining. This is what the EU citizens feel as well and they don't want to

---

3.   Eurostat publication 137/2007 12th October 2007
4.   Eurostat publication 140/2007 18th October 2007
5.   Eurostat publication 136/2007 11th October 2007

know why that is but they know that they are being lied to when EU Commissioner Joaquin Almunia is talking about "economic good times". All the growth Almunia celebrates as a big success in Eastern Europe is based on volume in retail trade, meaning that the mostly West German (very few French and British) shopping malls in the new member states are full of the West's top shelf products while the own industrial and agricultural production is sharply declining.

More tricks by the Barroso—Commission

But, the Barroso-Commission also ordered another change in the statistical methods being applied. In order not to show the ever greater disparity between classes of European society in the income statistics as well as in the household savings rate no longer the *medium* but the *median* figures are calculated. The medium figures would include the richest and the poorest quintiles whereas the median figures are reflecting only the middle class households. The growing gulf between rich and poor is not shown in these statistics. It nevertheless does exist and the reality is that the standard of living is declining for most citizens while everything becomes more expensive although the figures show a solid growth and a relatively low inflation. The latter of course only because the food basket that used to consist of some 200 goods now counts closer to 600 now containing electronic goods and household items which have relatively become cheaper and by this make up for the increase of products such as butter (+39% since 2001)[6] or fresh vegetables such as broccoli (+64.7%). One may not wish to buy a dish washer every day, but broccoli and other vegetables. It also would be acceptable if the wages were somewhat in line with the price rises but they are on a sharp decline in major economies such as Germany, Italy and France with for the first time ever after WWII the nominal *and* the net wages showing negative figures in 2004. In Germany, all the much celebrated up-swing (*Aufschwung*) is based on export, as domestic demand collapses due to constantly shrinking wages.

Above all, even the wage share dropped from 72.2% in 2000 to only 66.2% in 2006[7] as less than 60% of employments now being governed by the tariff scheme once negotiated between industries and the unions. Increasingly, normal jobs are replaced by "flexible" engagements by major recruitment agencies bearing only a minimal social security—, work protection—, health care- and pension standard. On top of that poverty is increasing drastically across the EU. More than 15% of

---

6.   Financial Times 26th September 2007
7.   Handelsblatt 27th June 2007

EU citizens were affected by severe poverty in 2004 while another 72 million Europeans are living with a high risk of poverty, according to the German financial daily Handelsblatt.[8]

This will increase dramatically although the EU Commission is eager not to report on this anymore as the poverty statistics have bee sacrificed over the Lisbon strategy against poverty which can only be seen as a cynical joke at this stage. Especially in Eastern Europe the decline becomes visible: All Eastern countries today have negative trade balances after they joined in 2004. Before, they enjoyed a somewhat balanced trade with the EU. Latest figures fro 2007 show the largest surplus to be accounted for by Germany (+114.9 billion €)[9], followed by the Netherlands (+23.6 billion €). The largest deficit was observed in the UK (-78.1 billion €) followed by Spain (-53.3 billion €), France (-22.9 billion €), Romania (-11.6 billion €) and Portugal (-10.1 billion €).

It becomes clear now, why the leadership of the EU, be it MEPs, EU governments or EU Commission officials want to eradicate the free, independent media: because we can find out and publish when they are lying in bed with the wrong bride.

Since the night of Lisbon it is a 'them and us' mentality

Most of the European citizens may not know much about the treaty or the draft constitution as they are not legal experts, economists, sociologists, but they sense that something is wrong. The average EU citizen may not be interested in the constitution or treaty and its militarization and police-state clauses as the ordinary law abiding citizen won't be affected by that. What the ordinary citizen indeed is affected by is the economic consequences of the agenda laid down in the treaty. It does make a difference to the ordinary citizen whether a certain social standard guarantees his survival in dignity or whether strict austerity criteria forces the governments to go with the chainsaw through the social net, cut down on pensions, health care, educational standards leaving public libraries, schools and universities under-funded. What kind of respect the political leadership of the EU has for the will of the people becomes evident when one listens to them carefully.

8.   Handelsblatt 19th May 2005
9.   Eurostat figures for January-July 2007, publication 141/2007 18th October 2007

"The substance of the constitution is preserved. That's a fact." German Chancellor Angela Merkel[10] in the European Parliament and here she is right. Nothing really has changed.

"The good thing about not calling it a constitution is that no one can ask for a referendum on it." said Guiliano Amato, vice-chairman of the convention that drew up the draft constitution at the London School of Economics.[11]

And even the most prominent advocate of Europeanism, the elder statesman Valerie Giscard d'Estaing, the chairman of the convention that drew up the constitution openly admitted that "In terms of content, the proposals remain largely unchanged, they are simply presented in a different way (...) The reason is that the new text could not look too much like the constitutional treaty (so EU governments agreed on) cosmetic changes to the constitution to make it easier to swallow."[12]

The majority of Europeans reject the neo-liberal agenda of the treaty of Lisbon that followed the draft constitution that fell through in the French and Dutch referenda.

It is only possible to govern against the will of the people by either an outright dictatorship (not fashionable these days) or by making the masses believe that it is in their interest. The latter is very difficult these days with all the digital multimedia around.

Under these circumstances it is only logic that one needs a streamlined media to hammer into the heads of the citizens that everything is alright. Now 300 TV channels are soon to tell us what a wonderful invention the EU is. So far they have managed quite well as although a majority of EU citizens is sceptical or even against the EU they do not see any alternative.

Private media conglomerates control already most of the member state's media with Rupert Murdoch owning some 40% of the media in the UK. In France, Vincent Bolloré, a good buddy of Nicolas Sarkozy whom he had lend his yacht to sail to Malta after the May election, accounts for more than 50% which he controls more or less directly. In Germany: the printed media, some 10,000 newspapers, are owned by 5 big hands: Springer, Bertelsmann, WAZ, Gruner & Jahr, Burda while each of them also holds significant shares in the private TV sector.

---

10.   27th June 2007
11.   20th February 2007
12.   17th July 2007 in the Constitutional Affairs committee of the European Parliament in Brussels

In Italy the cookie-monster, former Minister-president Silvio Berlusconi, wants to eat another TV station although everyone thought that he would not be able to run such a conglomerate from a prison cell and for that reason had held on to power so that Romano Prodi himself had to come with a saw and amputate the media tycoon from the throne after the elections. This not being enough of control over the media in the EU, the European Parliament is aiming to control the last niches of truly independent media.

Dr. Goebbel's wildest dreams come true. He has always dreamed of a centralised media that reaches everybody. To say that because I am free to say what I like proves that I am wrong is the threat with fascism.

PS. The park benches in the EU are no longer good for stretching out as they have little hobbles. In Eastern Europe one can still stretch out perfectly but that's maybe because in the past there were not that many people who would make use of it.

Banana RepEUblic

◆

Citizens left behind like Monkeys without Bananas

Lobbyism = Institutionalised Corruption

February 2008

In order to be awarded the status of a "Banana Republic" a state requires to have a small elite undermine its institutions and by this subordinate the government in order to push through their economic interests, or it simply has to sell bananas.

Because of the climate the EU is left with no other option but to have Lobbyists for various industries undermine the supposedly democratic institutions of the European Union as these usually do already quite successfully in *Western Free Democracies* and *New Europe* in the previously equally corrupted "Socialist" satellite states of the Soviets. In the latter, it is usually the same kind of elite with similar structures than in cold war times, in the West it is *always* the same elite, be it during the Kaiser era, the NAZIS or nowadays.

At present some 10,000 lobbyists are active in Brussels ensuring that things go the way their clients want it. The foremost successful although publicly almost unknown European Round Table of Industrialists (ERT) is the certainly most effective lobbying group. The ERT had been founded in 1983 and is certainly the most influential Lobbying group as it consists of 45 CEOs of major transnational corporations which all account for at least a billion Euros turnover such as Bayer, VEBA, Bosch, Daimler—Benz, Siemens, Bertelsmann, Krupp, Volvo, Thalys, Fiat, Phillips and others. The ERT members enjoy a unique access to the decision makers on the highest level in EU institutions as they also do on the various national levels in the Western Free Democracies. One of the biggest successes of the European Round Table of Industrialists has been the creation of a single market in connection with the Maastricht accord leading to the introduction of the Euro. But, also the trans European networks (TEN) for rail and road traffic, along with telecommunication knots which reach far into the North of Africa and the Maghreb region of the eastern Mediterranian sea, have to be seen in light of the economic interests these major corporations pursue. Most of these projects maybe to the benefit of Europeans as it improves the infrastructure and communication, leads to higher productivity and prosperity, although there is a downside as well. Major points on the ERT's wish-list for Santa Claus are social cuts, weaker environmental regulations and wide reaching deregulations and privatisations. Flexible workforce and low wages, lean state administrations who will have no power anymore to control what these majors are doing as well as a ruinous tax dumping competition are some of the less popular initiatives of Europe's real decision makers. But there are hundreds of other lobby groups as well, for instance EuropaBio, a company representing 500 European genetic technology companies whose aim is to lower the standards allowing manipulations like in the U.S. In reality, the course of the European Union today is effectively stirred by the 5 largest corporations of each field of business. This process started in the 1980ies when the EC Commission with some 300 laws eased tight laws in member states for mergers, fusions and takeovers from which trans-national corporations benefited immensely while SMEs producing for national markets suffered heavily.

But, who are the lobbyists? While Brussels became a kind of Capital of Europe, PR Agencies and „law firms" which in many cases act as Spin-doctors and not real legal advisors, but also journalists who transport the decisions in a way to the European citizens that they are either disinterested or disenfranchised and for this reason stop asking valid questions although they are directly affected, moved in a constant and never-ending stream to the Belgian capital. One of the major players in the PR lobbying is Burson-Marsteller, one of the worlds largest ones with 76 offices in 35 countries for which also US Senator Hillary Rodham Clinton used to work. Another one is Edelmann, founded in 1995, and representing mainly major corporations from the U.S., or Shandwick, a communications group "Master Media" company. These companies watch and influence the decision making process closely. No wonder that the citizens who are under-represented by only some 700 members of parliament feel neglected. But, well before, in the eighties, has the European Roundtable of Industrialists (ERT) institutionalised it's access to the decision makers in EC and later EU by creating the "Competitiveness Advisory Group".

According to a study by "Corporate Europe Observatory", a NGO in the Netherlands, over the past 20 years the ERT supports the EU Commission in abolishing national veto-rights although the noble club is not involved in detailed legislation or creation of directives but rather concentrates on setting forth the larger frame of EU decisions. The founding of the European Round Table of Industrialists antedates to the early 1980ies when the European Community seemed to be unable to deal with high inflation, high unemployment and declining growth rates. The VOLVO chief together with FIAT boss Umberto Agnelli and Wisse Dekker of Philips decided to take the initiative and lead 17 major industrialists to meet in April 1983 with EC Commissioners for Industries, Davignon and Finances, Ortoli, in order to create a club of the industrial elite of Europe like the Round Table of the US economy. The aim was to help the EC to advance and create a common market by eliminating trade barriers and harmonising regulations which ERT chairman Dekker proposed already in 1985. This proposal lead directly to the EUA (European Unified Act) or EEA accord. Dekker called his 5 year plan "Europe 1990: An Agenda for Action" and it only a few months later EC Commissioner for Industries Cockfield published a "White book" which later became the basis of the EUA. The only difference to Dekkert's ERT proposal was the timing. 1990 wasn't possible, also not so because of German unification, so it was 1992 when the common market became reality.

After the EUA became effective the European Round Table of Industrialists created a so called "Internal Market Support Committee" which between 1987 and 1992 held uncountable meetings with government and EC commission representatives in order to push through the realisation of the common market. EC Commission president Jacques Delors admitted in a TV interview in 1993 that there had been constant pressure by the ERT to launch the common market. After this has been achieved the ERT put it's next project on the agenda: the development of Europe's infrastructure. After the cold war had ended the idea to expand towards the East and by this increase profits by selling Western European goods to former Socialist states had been only a logic consequence. But, what would it be good to sell goods without getting these to the consumer? Megaprojects including the channel tunnel and Oresund bridge between Denmark and Sweden were already under way, but what about Eastern Europe? 12,000 kilometres of new motorways and high speed trains were planned and eventually also being built.

Parallel to this the ERT pushed for the introduction of a single currency, arguing (as early as 1985) that the whole mechanism of a common market would be quite useless if there were still different national monetary policies. In its proposal

"Reshaping Europe" dating back to spring 1991, the European Roundtable of Industrialists proclaimed a schedule for the "European Monetary Union" (EMU) in almost exactly the same manner as it later, in December 1991, became the official version of the *Maastricht Accord*. Another example for the excellent cooperation between non-elected (super-) state officials and the industrial elite of Europe can be seen in the publication of Jacques Delors' famous white book "Growth, Competitiveness, Employment" in 1993 which had been edited by the ERT suggesting "deregulation, flexible labour markets, investments into transport infrastructure and international competitiveness" all of which we find in the so called "Lisbon Strategy of Stability & Growth". Current priorities for the ERT are still the enhancing of competitiveness and the benchmarking, meaning that the most capital—friendly lowest international level shall become the standard in Europe, as well as the Eastern Expansion. ERT chairman Richardson already said in 1997 that the expansion into the East offered 150 million new consumers, low wages and a highly qualified workforce, in other words "a new South East Asia at our doorstep."

50 more years?

✦

EU Treaty Overkill—Citizens sceptical—Funeral March European Round Table of Industrialists finally succeeds

03ʳᵈ December 2007

Where does the unification of Europe in it's 50th year stand today as the EU treaty, which replaces this week the "Constitution" which had fallen through in one referendum after the other despite being heavily championed by the European Round Table of Industrialists (ERT), and the German government in particular and will it last?

The Financial Times published on 14th July of this year an opinion poll according to which only a quarter of the EU citizens of the five largest EU countries say that the EU had improved their lives. 44% instead see a decline in their standard of living. But, leaving the EU is also not seen as an option. Only 22% think that this is a good option.

It should make political leaders who gather this week in Lisbon for the signing of the EU treaty which has been agreed to replace the draft constitution worry that the citizens are not in a mood to celebrate with the heads of state and governments. EU citizens are not only not really interested in EU affairs, but as the Financial Times found in a poll it published on 26th September 2007 are in their vast majority disenfranchised with the economic system which almost 70% seem to find not holding much in store for themselves. The majority of citizens asked across Europe also expressed concern that the EU could be in danger to copy the US's economic model. The most distinctive advocate for such an approach was until recently French President Nicolas Sarkozy who had won over his conditioner washed socialist opponent Ségolène Royal on the back of media tycoon

Vincent Boloré who also owns and controls other CAC 40—listed major industries in France, such as in the defence and construction sector.

A Bear—Hug

The times of Konrad Adenauer and Charles de Gaulle making France and West-Germany become the motor for European integration are history and also the pragmatic cooperation between Helmut Schmidt and Valerie de Giscard d'Estaing or the hand-holding ceremonies over the graves of WWI soldiers in Verdun of Helmut Kohl and Francoise Mitterrand belong to the past. Today, Europe is probably more split than ever before over how to continue although the division seems to have been overcome. In fact, the latter can be a misconception and provide for a hard landing for the leaders when they learn that the citizens don't follow them at all. France and Germany have never been farer away from each other and the UK, always being a bit on the sidelines, only reluctantly agreed to the treaty.

The truth is that neither France nor the UK got much out of the EU expansion and are seemingly not getting much from the EU treaty either. That's why Britain got a few special conditions written in which rather appear to be 'opt-out clauses'. France was not able to negotiate properly after the Franco-German brotherhood had been taken it's breath by the hug of the Berliner bear.

The German industry already dominates a large portion of the French economic output and was attempting to take over the Energy conglomerates of France. In an unusual departure from his otherwise neo-classical agenda Nicolas Sarkozy acted as a state-interventionist when ordering the fusion of Electricité de France and Gaz de France. It is clear that this step by the French president as much as it is against his own convictions is directed against a potential take-over bid by the Germans. Having also fought vigorously over the French stakes in EADS and Airbus Sarkozy is left with the task to rescue France from Germany. Charles De Gaulle would turn in his grave if he saw what and how Sarkozy was doing it.

"The German problem antedates World War I", the International Herald Tribune wrote[1] a few years ago. "It is not just an affair of NAZISM and WWII; it goes back to the Franco-Prussian war and German unification in 1871. When Bismarck brought all but Austria undessa's domination, the German state was the

---

1.   7th December 2000

most populous in Europe. It was too big. It unbalanced the old Europe, over-shadowing France and Austria-Hungary, and challenging the British Empire." That's exactly where we stand again, after two world wars and the cold war being over, by neither side carrying a permanent victory, one can be tempted to think as the Communist system imploded while the capitalistic system seems to explode starting one war after another over natural resources while the financial system is collapsing.

It started with the Steel-Union

All what Adenauer and de Gaulle had negotiated in 1951 was about coal and steel, but it was more: it was about the new equilibrium in Europe. It laid the ground for increasing cooperation, first economically, then politically, and it did not take long until one spoke about the French-German brotherhood becoming a driving force for the unification of Europe. All these decades it had been essential to the few European nations being involved that all members be treated as equals, no matter what size or how populous. This was the equilibrium that made the French, Dutch, Belgians and Luxemburgers gain confidence in the new (West-) Germany. Having suffered tremendously from previous German expansions, those nations have been very wary of any attempt by the Germans to fall back into hegemony-power behaviour. It probably helped at this stage that Germany was divided and not sovereign. The two Germanies were rivals from the very beginning, and the East-German socialist state by it's sheer existence may have been responsible for a more socially balanced and in it's foreign affairs modest West—Germany. In fact, the latter was probably the Germany liked better, as it was a non-repressive, liberal society, abstaining not only because of the cold war but also because of a general mood in Germany from any military adventurism. All this changed after 3rd October 1990, and the promises of chancellor Helmut Kohl and foreign minister Hans-Dietrich Genscher that "only peace shall come from German soil" were soon forgotten. The Herald Tribune noted that "Germany's venture into policy leadership in 1992, by forcing EU recognition of Croatia and Slovenia did not prove a good idea".[2] To put it mildly, other European leaders were not amused by foreign minister Hans-Dietrich Genscher combining German approval of the Maastricht accord with a European vote on it's policy towards the new—old—Yugoslavian republics who were about to trigger the first war in Europe since 1945. I remember how French foreign minister

---

2.   dito

Roland Dumas stormed out of the conference room in the Maastricht castle fuming and uttering that he doesn't want to be blackmailed. He later told me that he was upset about the German delegation who said they would refuse to sign the treaty leading to the European Monetary Union which later resulted in the single currency, the Euro, if France did not recognise Croatia and Slovenia diplomatically. Should the agreement signed at Maastricht survive only the following days it would be necessary for Europe to speak with a single voice in the emerging Balkan conflict, the German side argued, meaning that chancellor Helmut Kohl's promise of "full diplomatic recognition of Croatia and Slovenia before Christmas"[3] buried any hope for a peaceful solution in the conflict. Even the liberal weekly DIE ZEIT admitted that "the splitting-up of the Yugoslavian state, along with the closer alignment of the Croats and Slovenians with the German economy, brought kind of an emancipation of these peoples who had previously been attached to the empires in central Europe and later with the 'Third Reich', but also meant to be a punishment for the Serbs, who have been on the victor's side in both world wars. And thirdly, it also made those treaties vanish which punished Germany for it's two defeats. In short: due to the almighty economy, Germany regained what it lost in battle."[4] US Secretary of State Warren Christopher openly criticised the government in Bonn by saying that "All the process of granting diplomatic recognition to Croatia and Slovenia contained serious mistakes and the Germans bear a special responsibility for that."[5]

France's miscalculation

Today, when the 50th anniversary of the treaty of Rome is commemorated and the new treaty which is replacing the draft "constitution" which can only be seen as an ill-advised attempt to impose an imperialistic rule on the peoples of Europe a lot more is at stake than a institutional reform. Germany has economically achieved what Hitler couldn't by military brutality, terrorism and torture. By becoming too pushy, Germany may overkill it, though. Doubts are raised everywhere whether the European Union will exist for much longer than when the EU treaty that is signed today comes into effect.

What chancellor Helmut Schmidt and President Valerie de Giscard d'Estaigne, German unification-chancellor Helmut Kohl and President Francoise

---

3.   Deutscher Bundestag 15th December 1991
4.   DIE ZEIT 24th January 1999
5.   USA TODAY 28th January 1999

Mitterrand had lived up for now is at stake. France tried to control Germany and only reluctantly gave it's blessing for German unification in 1990 being assured that Germany's military forces would only be used for defending German soil. And, Francoise Mitterrand has been assured by Helmut Kohl that the Germans would only seek expansion within the framework of the European Community, now the European Union. But, the French were daydreaming if they really thought that they could if not control Germany but at least keep it somewhat under control. ECB president Jean-Claude Trichet is a Frenchman, yes, but 2/3 of his staff are former Bundesbank employees.

After all, that's why the ECB is situated in Frankfurt am Main and not in Lyon, Paris or Strasbourg.

Economic principles still the same as in the draft 'constitution'

The economic agenda of the European Union will be as neo-liberal as the Maastricht accord in the early nineties defined "economic stability" as a fiscal austerity that forced those countries adopting the EURO to commit to a crackdown on social, cultural and ecological standards. As if our political leaders haven't learnt a lesson from the 1990ies during which the virtual reality casino of the stock markets, new technology "boom" and fraudulent financial markets created an incredible unemployment as well as a new gulf between rich and poor leading us into a crisis as serious as between the two world wars, they try to let this neo-liberal agenda appear to be inevitable and without alternative. In the constitution's article III-69 they were subscribing to an "unrestricted free market governed by competition" which abides to the principles laid by the governmental conference in June 2004. As this has in the due course become hugely unpopular with the vast majority of the citizens smelling even before the financial crisis kicking off on August 11th that something was wrong, the German presidency avoided mentioning the economic principles owners of industries and shareholders were dictating the political leadership of Europe. Instead, a side note to the treaty was agreed on, having the same content but be hidden behind the framework of the treaty at a far less prominent but still as effective position.

The principles laid down in the treaty's annex describe the "Growth & Stability Pact" and the contained price stability as the *ultima ratio*. The rest pretty much remained the same as well. In Article I-3 of the draft constitution the "Cultural diversity as well as Arts" have been reduced to a minimum, just in line with the WTO regulations (III-55). The fight against unemployment would be subordinated to the overall economic policy (III-100) and governed by the one-sided orientation of the European Central Bank on their principle of price stability (Article I-29) as well as the "Stability Pact" (Art. III-76). Overall, all this has stayed pretty much the same in the treaty.

Another crucial aspect is taxation. Only the indirect taxes, such as VAT, Petrol—, Alcohol, Luxury-Goods Tax etc. shall be harmonised but not the income and corporate taxes. Therefore, the ruining process of tax dumping will be further reinforced. Major corporations will continue to follow the mere logic of investing only in those countries of dwindling tax rates. Member states continue to compete with each other (or break up like Great-Britain which for the simple reason of tax dumping competition have 'independence' movements in Scotland and Wales which for only that reason are supported by industries in the UK) in lowering corporate taxes and in the end no taxes will be paid by those rich multinational corporations and stock market listed companies who often received structural funds and subsidies from Brussels, the tax payers pay and by this encourage those beneficiaries to further cut down employment as well as labour—, social- and ecological standards.

Thus, the EU Constitution was and the treaty replacing it now is falling back well behind what the West-German constitution, the Basic Law, still holds up as a key goal: a socially balanced free market with no exclusions of public ownership where beneficial or necessary. This has been for four decades the success model of West-Germany as it has been guaranteeing social rights *and* free entrepreneurship, all relatively well balanced. It will be difficult to explain to the German people why this has to be given up now, especially since the disastrous consequences of an unregulated Manchester Capitalism becomes more and more obvious. But not only the West Germans will miss their relatively liberal and human rights focused Basic Law but also East Germans who traditionally enjoyed much more social rights until unification. In their eyes the so called western free democracies and their economic system may further loose credibility and acceptance.

European Expansion—Tabula Rasa in Eastern Europe

While we heard a lot about the so called East-West divide in Europe finally to be overcome and East European countries being brought back into the family of Western democracies the financial daily Handelsblatt[6] concentrated in the for their readers important question how these can maximise the profit of their inherited or somehow collected millions and billions. The news that the expansion of the EU towards the east would create the biggest profits in the German portfolios certainly encouraged Germany's shareholders to invest in DAX—listed corporations rather than in EUROSTOXX DJ 50 multinational companies. The reason for this was simple: the EUROSTOXX DJ 50 listed companies were expecting a growth in return on investment by 17% while the DAX listed corporations were expecting to gain some 50% or more after they accumulated 30% in the year before (2003). This incredible growth was only partly be owed to the crack down on the social system and everything Schröder called "painful but necessary reforms" but especially to the expansion towards the East. As Germany's industry had been suffering from an expansion crisis the collapse of the trade barriers have so far been quite beneficial in particular to the DAX listed German retailers as well as financial institutions and car manufacturers. On the one hand the expectations were high in terms of consumption but on the other hand also for reducing production costs due to much lower labour costs which are in many cases only a fraction of those of Germany or any other West European country. An hour of work in Lithuania for instance costs only 2.42 €, in Estonia 3.03 €, in Poland 4.48 €, in Slovenia 8.98 € including social costs. Compared to West European costs of roughly 20 € per hour it became a great field for speculation and profit maximisation. Not only did this lead to a job transfer towards the East and by this let unemployment in the "old" EU hit the ceiling but also to the collapse of medium sized companies in the East which can not compete with the wholesalers and major production companies from the West. Also, many farmers in the new member states are ruined as they couldn't compete with the highly subsidised agricultural sector of the West European countries. And, it had been made crystal clear to Poland that they won't get the same financial support for their farmers like the Irish, French, Austrian and other "old" members for decades got. This may explain why Poland was so reluctant to give it's blessing for the treaty. Moreover, the West German retailers did not only open their supermarket chains in the East but also provide the products, a situation we have already observed when the German Democratic Republic (GDR) was taken over by West Germany in 1990. Without a single shot being fired, the West German industries all of a sudden had a new market which they dominate.

---

6.   Handelsblatt 29th March 2004 „DAX Titel profitieren von Ost-Erweiterung"

Expansion nothing but a change of ownership

In contrast to the kind of 'hostile take-over' in 1990 we can say that this process was already well under way for several years when East European state holdings were privatised and in most cases sold to West European "investors". In the financial sector of Poland and Czech Republic one can say that more than 70% of the banks are now owned by the West European banks, in Hungary 60% and in Slovakia 80%. German wholesaler Metro and car manufacturers like VW and Audi are aggressively gaining significant market shares.

But the EU expansion not only means that West European companies and shareholders are benefiting from profit maximisation but also receive the bulk of the EU subsidies paid to the new member states. This leads to the perverse situation that the taxpayers in West European countries finance the transfer of jobs to the East while in the new member states the medium sized manufacturers and retailers are ruined. Agricultural as well as industrial production is on a sharp decline in all new member states while the double digit growth rates let EU Economic Affairs Commissioner Joaquin Almunia become indulgent. But, the "growth" is only happening in the retail sector, meaning that citizens in the East are all consuming top shelf products produced in the West while their own industries are at best degraded to providing cheap labour.

The only ones to gain from this blunt mercantile boom are the West European major corporations, especially those listed in the DAX. The labour costs and wages in West European countries as a consequence are further under pressure and therefore will continue to shrink to a minimum. On the contrary, in the East European countries we don't see a rise in income and wealth but in the number of EU subsidised cheap labour and also unemployment and a social disaster as due to the steadily decreasing corporate taxes the state's pockets are empty in those countries as well. In other words, the same development can be foreseen as in Germany after Schröder's tax-reform. It is ridiculous in this regard that the mega tax-dumper now criticises the new tax-dumpers in Eastern Europe but that's why Schröder had been labelled Europe's leading *reformist*. The hypocrisy is unrivalled. A European tax harmonisation could have been agreed on but one neither heard Schröder and Blair nor chancellor Angela Merkel, President Nicolas Sarkozy or Prime Minister Gordon Brown even suggest such initiative to prevent a tax dumping competition among the member countries.

One could for instance have agreed on a minimum corporate tax rate across Europe rather than the unhealthy Maastricht "stability" pact. "Everybody as an average becomes richer", concludes the Handelsblatt in it's editorial. That is true. On an average basis always everybody will be richer but the same one could say about the world economy. For some reason "on an average basis" does not mean that the majority does not get poorer while the top ten thousand shareholders on this planet become richer and richer, especially after the new EU members have been "allowed" entry into the noble club of the EU. This may be the main reason why Europe's citizens are more than sceptical about what Merkel, Sarkozy and their friends of the "European Round Table of Industrialists" are cooking.

Oui, Monsieur le Génèrale ...

Somewhere in Heaven, Konrad Adenauer and Charles de Gaulle sit together and observe on a TV screen the funeral ceremony of Lisbon. Let's listen for a few moments to the comments of these icons of European Unification.

"Did you see that, Monsieur le Chancellier? They are really going to sign the treaty, they will sell our industries to "les Bouches"[1] the old man with the cylinder-like military cap and grey moustache said.

"Ah, no, Monsieur le Président, it's all right. You know, it's the Franco-German brotherhood, we are all brothers, so it stays in the family!" the man sitting next to him replied staring at the big plasma screen. For hours the various TV channels were showing images of the EU Summit in Lisbon where the 'mini' constitution, the so called *reform treaty*, was signed in a ceremony that rather appeared like a funeral.

"Brothers! Ha, that's what you wished we were, Monsieur Kanzler, but that can maybe be said about you and me. We were made from a different wood than those ones!" Charles de Gaulle replied angrily pointing at the big plasma TV screen in front of them.

"Times have changed, I'd say. We have to let the young generations do it their way." Konrad Adenauer said.

"But not the same mistakes the generations before us have made. France has been on the victor's side of the two world wars!" de Gaulle retorted and the way his big nose blew when he said it would make one fear that he was ready to go into battle again.

"But Monsieur le Génèrale, I think we have for a long time overcome those differences. Haven't we both launched the coal and steel union together so that we share the resources to the mutual benefit of our nations?" Konrad Adenauer gave back.

General de Gaulle stared at the ceiling.

---

1. „the pigs"; some French used to call the Germans because of the NAZI occupation like that. Understandable after all that had happened.

"And, Monsieur le Générale, hasn't this created the European Community?" the German chancellor insisted.

"Yes, Monsieur Chancellier, it has, but it had gotten out of hand."

"Ah you mean because of German unification, but you have to understand that it is the right of every people to live in it's own statehood."

"Of course, that's why Mitterrand agreed to it. But the idea was that the unified Germany like the good old RFA[2] would be still the same modest, peace loving, good neighbour."

"So it is and always will be, Monsieur le Générale." Konrad Adenauer replied looking a bit distraught by his French counterpart's underlying tone.

"Well, my dear Herr Kanzler, that can hardly be said. It was Hans-Dietrich Genscher and Helmut Kohl who combined their approval of the Maastricht accord in 1991 leading to the monetary union and later the Euro with the diplomatic recognition of these Yugoslavian self declared mini-republics just to regain economically what Germany lost in battle in the two world wars."

"Ah, no, mon chere Générale, let's not start with that. At the same time the *force de frappe*[3] was still directed at German cities although your successors were speaking of the Franco-Allemande brotherhood. Come-on, that discussion won't lead us anywhere. We Germans sacrificed our beloved Deutsche Mark in order to be good Europeans."

"But you see who benefited most from it: Germany has a trade surplus of 97 billion, France a trade deficit of 30 billion Euros."

"That can hardly be seen as our fault." Adenauer replied and leaned back in his armchair.

"Truth be told is that our people see the Euro as some kind of *Reichsmark*. And, it is mostly German industries, retailers and banks which conquer the markets in Eastern Europe" De Gaulle insisted.

"Now you are really becoming funny, Monsieur le Générale, the president of the central bank is a Frenchman!" the old German chancellor threw back at the man who had fought in the Résistance.

"But why is it in Frankfurt and not in Lyon, Herr Kanzler?!" de Gaulle retorted.

"Because our weapon manufacturers have moved there and even had to sacrifice EADS and Airbus, non, Monsieur, there is nothing unbalanced.

---

2.   République Fédérale d'Allemagne (West-Germany)

3.   France's nuclear defense system

"But yet, it is not like it used to be, Monsieur Adenauer." Charles de Gaulle replied looking angrily at his finger nails.

"What do you mean? We are partners. We are friends."

"You and me, yes, we had a different vision but look what happens now: Électricité de France and Gaz de France have to merge just to fight off a take over bid by the German energy conglomerates although it was always said that '*liberalisation*' would lead to unbundled networks but this must have gone lost in the translation." General de Gaulle complained. Konrad Adenauer stared at the ceiling.

"And," the General went on "'*modernisation*' should mean to reach a higher standard of production but instead the 'Stability & Growth Pact' forces us to crack down on any social standard and labour law. Germany forces us to break with any tradition France was made strong by. Friends wouldn't do that to each other."

A few moments of absolute silence followed. Both men stared at the screen in front of them.

"Maybe you are right, Monsieur le Générale, it is as you said before: we had a different vision." Konrad Adenauer with a breaking voice said. Charles de Gaulle didn't turn his head to look at his friend but just took his hand and held it for a moment. There it was again, the understanding between the two great leaders. Without words. Just in his mind the general thought that maybe it had been a mistake to have Saarlouis with all it's steel industry be allowed to join West-Germany in 1953, but he eliminated those thoughts quickly again.

All of a sudden something caught both men's attention.

"What is she doing there?" Konrad Adenauer asked pointing at Lady Margaret Thatcher who in a red costume carrying her famous black handbag at her right arm while pulling with her left arm Prime Minister Gordon Brown up the stairs to the conference centre.

"I thought she had left office 20 years ago?" the German chancellor asked.

"Yes, but didn't you hear her say a few weeks ago when she paid a visit to No.10, that her greatest success was to create New Labour?"

"Yes, I remember, but why is she here now, well there, rather?"

"Brown needs her to keep Cameroon at bay. It really upset the Tories that she had tea with Brown."

"But does that mean that Gordon Brown now needs his nanny to follow him everywhere?"

"She is not following she was already there." the General very dryly remarked, then the two old men concentrated on the screen again.

They observed how the Iron Lady energetically pulled the right arm of Britain's longest serving Prime Minister-in-waiting shouting at him 'you go up there and you tell them to stick their treaty wherever they want but not into our backyard! We are not going to surrender to Frankfurt, tell them!'. Gordon Brown did not look happy. 'But, Madam, that wouldn't be very diplomatic' the British Prime Minister carefully said but the old baroness only pulled her right arm and knocked her handbag over the head of the Prime Minister who tried to duck away but got hit anyway. 'Ouch!' he screamed as hundreds of pebble stones fell out of the Iron Lady's handbag.

"Ha!" General de Gaulle roared, did you see that, it was full of *Northern Pebbles*! I always had wondered what she was carrying there, it could not have been lipstick, that's what I knew."

"I bet you were not the only one who wondered." Konrad Adenauer replied pointing at Helmut Kohl who was walking in saluting and waving to all sides. A few steps behind him came Angie Merkel.

"He is a good *garcon* your grandson." General de Gaulle remarked.

"He is not my grandson, he always said so, but I know it better."

"You should undergo a DNA test, Monsieur Adenauer."

"I never met his grandmother." Konrad Adenauer, visibly not amused, insisted.

"Ha, who knows!" De Gaulle replied with a twinkle in his eye.

"I swear to the almighty God that I don't know that woman!" Adenauer shouted with his cheeks gaining colour due to his excitement.

"Now, you sound like Clinton!" the old general gave back dryly.

Then, they listened to Helmut Kohl's address:

"I was not only the father of German Unity but also of European Unification and I say that very clearly to all of you so that there can not be any misunderstanding: there is no way back but many ways forward. It is now for you, the young generation, to find your way. It is your future, it is your Europe." the father of the unification of Europe said to the audience consisting of politicians who were at best fathers and mothers if not grandparents while at the same time outside the conference centre the "Europe's Future", young students were clashing with the Portuguese police who were forcefully dissolving a so far peaceful demonstration of students from all across Europe demanding that public universities deemed being ineffective were not shut down and privatised.

The next one to enter the podium was the French President N.Sarkozy (Narkozy): "What has been begun by Konrad Adenauer and Charles de Gaulle after the second world war, has now been brought to a conclusion. The European Union advances as the United States of Europe!"

De Gaulle looked disgusted. His hand reached for the Cognac bottle on the little table between Adenauer and himself.

"When he gets here I will wash his head!" the General uttered as he poured himself a decent zip.

Then, it was the moment José Manuel Barroso (JMB) has waited for all the time. He jumped up the stairs to the stage and spread his charm.

"As the president of Europe, let me emphasise that we are today celebrating the formation of the non-imperialistic empire of independent European nations...." JMB said and back in Heaven both old men just stare at each other.

"Who is he, now, for God's sake and why is he saying he was the president of Europe?!" General de Gaulle fumed.

Then, the Son of God came in. Don't forget where you are, the Son of God said as he had overheard the last sentence when he entered the room. "Come-on gentlemen, we are ready to go to bed." the man with the long beard said and switched off the big plasma screen.

"Better here than down there!" mumbled the old general as he slowly got off from his armchair. "We won't send you back anyhow." the Son of God replied with a huge smile on his face.

P.S. unfortunately, the scenes reported on here were not be made available by major broadcasters, that's why you couldn't see it with your own eyes. Only people in heaven could …

978-0-595-49205-3
0-595-49205-3